PRAISE FOR
THE FLIGHT TO EXCELLENCE

"Captain "T"—the quintessential Renaissance man—has done it yet again. He's taken a trajectory outside his core flight plan as a pilot, lawyer, businessman, government official, civic leader, philanthropist, and motivational commentator to develop a world-class primer on personal development and business success. As he is himself "a man for all seasons," so too is this tome a vital handbook for folks in all stages of personal development to employ his mechanisms to jet to their destiny."

—**Fletcher "Flash" Wiley,** General Counsel and Former Chairman,
Boston Chamber of Commerce and Director, TJX Companies

"Don't just read this book; use it as your daily flight plan. William "T" Thompson doesn't write about life truths; instead, he reveals the principles he lived by to achieve a life of excellence. In a world with few role models, he is one I am constantly learning from."

—**Barry Banther,** Author of *A Leader's Gift: How to Earn the
Right to Be Followed*, Hall of Fame Speaker, and Chairman
of the Board of the National Speakers Association

"Wow! What a great leadership book that I had trouble putting down. It was *that* good! My friend and classmate "T" Thompson has written a book that will make a profound difference in your personal and professional life. His book is a must-read!"

—**Steve Lorenz,** President, The Falcon Foundation and
Retired USAF 4-Star General

"The compelling principles espoused in this book fit the Captain's life to a "T" (pun intended)! It amply demonstrates that striving for excellence in all that one does is truly the key to success in all phases of life."

—**Wayne A. Budd,** Former Associate Attorney General of the United States and Chairman, AAA

"*The Flight to Excellence*, written in "T"s insightful and direct style, clearly shows how consistently applying his *Principles, People, Flight Plan*, and *Performance* concepts can lead to both personal and business success. I found that in revealing his personal story, he prompted me to reflect on my own story, thereby causing me to more consciously focus on these practical and simple, but in the end transformational, principles. I highly recommend it."

—**Hugh Williamson,** Fortune 500 Chairman, CEO, and Serial Entrepreneur

"I highly recommend "T" Thompson's book *The Flight to Excellence*. The book brilliantly conveys practical and valuable advice in a way that is both inspirational and attainable. I've worked with literally hundreds of young professionals of color as the CEO of The Partnership, a leadership development organization in Boston. These professionals yearn for role models and tactics to grow and thrive in their careers and lives. If I were still in that role, *The Flight to Excellence* would be required reading and "T" Thompson would be an annual guest speaker."

—**Bennie Wiley,** Corporate Director and Former CEO

"Captain "T" has written a powerful guide to not only help you get clear on what you want in life, but he then gives you the strategy to ensure you get there. His personal stories and his well-thought-out plan make this a must-read for anyone just starting their career or those of us on the tail end looking to create our legacy. Love this book!"

—**Meridith Elliott Powell,** Award-Winning Author of *Own It: Redefining Responsibility*, Top 15 Business Growth Expert, and Keynote Speaker

"As our country finally has its critical conversation on race, Captain "T" demonstrates in his new book how excellence overcomes these obstacles and leads to sustained success. Most importantly, he shows the reader how they can do it too. A must-read in these times."

—**Greg Moore,** Former Managing Editor,
The Boston Globe and *The Denver Post*

"*Integrity First, Service Before Self, and Excellence in All We Do.* These are the core values of the Air Force Academy where "T" Thompson and I went to school. This book clearly shows how consistently applying these values leads to personal, business, and even financial success."

—**John Regni,** 17th Superintendent, USAF Academy
and Retired USAF 3-Star General

"An outstanding leadership tool at a time when it is desperately needed. This book shows how excellence is a choice and can be a tremendous competitive advantage at a time when mediocrity has become the commodity of the day."

—**Dick McConn,** Chairman of the National Defense
Industry Association and CEO of M International Inc.

"Leading during turbulence requires a moral compass to stay on course. Captain "T" clearly provides a flight manual with his P4 System on how to do this for sustained excellence and enduring impact."

—**Dana H. Born,** Chair, Senior Executive Fellows (SEF) Program,
Center for Public Leadership, Harvard University, Kennedy School of
Government, and Retired USAF Brigadier General

"Captain "T"'s P4 System for success is built around integrity, good people skills, attention to detail, and not forgetting where he came from. If a young African American kid from segregated South Carolina born to teenage parents can use this simple system as a blueprint for his success, everyone can use it as a guide to his or her own success. His ability to incorporate his life experiences into principles for success is outstanding and is well worth the read."

—**George Brooks,** President, UPS International, Inc. Americas

"Captain "T"'s story is incredibly compelling, and his insights guide all of us to embrace excellence in our own lives. *The Flight to Excellence* is a roadmap that will enrich any life. I love this book!"

—**Mark Scharenbroich,** Emmy Award Winner,
Hall of Fame Speaker, and Award-Winning Author of *Nice Bike*

"This book is timely as our country finally has the difficult conversation on justice and race that we have needed for so long. Captain "T" has excelled as a leader with the courage to live by the Air Force core values we share: *Integrity First, Service Before Self, and Excellence in All We Do*. He has demonstrated how consistently applying the P4 System has achieved sustained success despite historic challenges. Most importantly, "T" shows how you can do it too."

—**Michelle Johnson,** 19th Superintendent, USAF Academy,
First Woman to Lead a U.S. Department of Defense
Service Academy, and Retired 3-Star General

"This is a masterpiece for businesses and individuals who are tired of circling the airport of uncertainty and ready to land the plane by excelling in excellence. The P4 System is simple, substantive, and a fresh way of thinking in this transformative period in history. I'm recommending this book to everyone I know. It's a must-read!"

—**Simon T. Bailey,** Author of *Shift Your Brilliance*
and Hall of Fame Speaker

SOARING *to* NEW HEIGHTS
IN BUSINESS *and* LIFE

THE

FLIGHT

TO

EXCELLENCE

== CAPTAIN ==

WILLIAM "T" THOMPSON, ESQ.

GREENLEAF
BOOK GROUP PRESS

Published by Greenleaf Book Group Press
Austin, Texas
www.gbgpress.com

Distributed by Greenleaf Book Group

For ordering information or special discounts for bulk purchases, please contact Greenleaf Book Group at PO Box 91869, Austin, TX 78709, 512.891.6100.

Design and composition by Greenleaf Book Group
Cover design by Greenleaf Book Group
Cover Image: ©Mega Pixel, used under license from Shutterstock.com

Publisher's Cataloging-in-Publication data is available.

Print ISBN: 978-1-62634-746-5

eBook ISBN: 978-1-62634-747-2

Part of the Tree Neutral® program, which offsets the number of trees consumed in the production and printing of this book by taking proactive steps, such as planting trees in direct proportion to the number of trees used: www.treeneutral.com

Printed in the United States of America on acid-free paper

20 21 22 23 24 25   10 9 8 7 6 5 4 3 2 1

First Edition

To my Momma Pearl; my daughters, Taylor and Sydney; my life partner, Le Yen; and my sisters, Tina and Denise—all the women in my life who have made me a better man.

And to my dad, who since August 29, 2016, has looked down on me from above and is still the shining light that guides me every day.

CONTENTS

ACKNOWLEDGMENTS

TO THE PEOPLE WHO HAVE SHAPED MY LIFE

Orangeburg, South Carolina:
To my first best friends—James "Warkii" Sulton and Melissa Evans (my next-door neighbor). Though I was there first, they later joined me at Orangeburg High and also lived some of the stories in this book. Over six decades later, they are still my homeboy and homegirl.

=====

United States Air Force Academy, Colorado Springs, Colorado:
Herb Harrison and "O" Mitchell, my best friends in life. We met during our first summer at the Academy and have been the closest of friends ever since. They have always been there for me, even in the toughest of times, and I am blessed to have such remarkable relationships.

=====

Moody Air Force Base, Valdosta, Georgia:
Captain Larry Strothers and Lieutenant (now Major General [Ret.]) Felix Dupre. These are the guys who taught me how to fly—Captain Strothers in the T-37 and "the Dupe" in the T-38.

They made a challenging pilot training program fulfilling and fun. These gents were the foundation of my aviation career.

=====

Mather Air Force Base, Sacramento, California:
Mr. Charles Siplin. Charles was the big brother I never had. Though only five years older, he became my mentor and taught me a lot about "class." He introduced me to wealth and power and the finer things in life.

=====

Boston, Massachusetts:
Fletcher "Flash" Wiley, Air Force Academy class of 1965. My second big brother, power broker, and bon vivant. He is also my best friend, and you will read some about him in this book.

Wayne Budd, lawyer extraordinaire, who has served at the highest levels of government and corporate America, yet never forgot where he came from. He brought me into the Sunday Morning Basketball Group, some of the finest guys I have ever known.

Lori Stoico, my executive assistant at the Summit Group. When I was in the air, Lori always made the right call on the ground. To all my employees at all of the Summit Group Companies—your efforts made the companies' successes possible.

Richard Taylor and Jim Brannon. They brought me into the National Association of Guardsmen, an organization that is like no other on the planet, and that is no exaggeration!

=====

Association of Graduates (AOG), USAF Academy:

Bob Munson, classmate and member of the association's board of directors. The absolute best board member who I have ever had the honor of serving with, and I have served on thirty corporate and nonprofit boards. The graduate community owes him a great debt of gratitude.

Steve Lorenz, classmate, retired four-star general, and partner in crime. We ran symbiotic organizations for the benefit of the Academy and the graduate community. Our friendship helped us move the ball forward during some challenging times.

Gary Howe and Marty Marcolongo, my top two lieutenants at the AOG. These guys implemented the vision that took the AOG to new heights and engaged the graduates like never before. They were the leaders of a great team.

Brigadier General (Ret.) Roger Carleton and Terry Storm, my board chairs for most of my time as president and CEO. They were great to work with and understood the nature of a strategic board.

Atlanta, Georgia:

My fellow members of the Atlanta Guardsmen, a rowdy, fun-loving but classy group of guys.

The Archons of Delta Upsilon Boulé and my fellow members of the 100 Blackmen of Atlanta. Great organizations, great guys doing great work for the community.

Leadership Atlanta—Pat, Laura, the rest of the staff, and all my fellow alumni. It is a fantastic program, and I will be a volunteer until you roll me away.

And finally to my friends and colleagues at Greenleaf Book Group: Justin, Sally, Jen, Karen, and the rest of the group. Thank you all for helping me get this done. Hopefully it will be just the beginning of a long and fruitful relationship.

INTRODUCTION

> *"I am the master of my fate:*
> *I am the captain of my soul."*
>
> —WILLIAM ERNEST HENLEY,
> English poet

YOU ARE SITTING at your desk, *thinking*—actually *thinking* for a change. It's something that you usually have little time for—because ordinarily you are so busy *doing*. Your normal daily requirements are nonstop, but you still often feel that you're not accomplishing enough (or fast enough) to get you where you think you should be. You're smart, you do the work, and you are dedicated, but you're just not flying as high as you know you can.

Welcome to the club. This is an all-too-common feeling among many business executives, professionals, and entrepreneurs. They feel they are making the sacrifices, working long hours, and putting in the effort, but they sense their return on investment is often mediocre at best. The problem is not your intelligence or your commitment. And it certainly is not your ambition, because you want to be considered among the elite. The difficulty is often not having a laser-like focus on exactly what you are striving for and not having a proven process that enables you to distinguish yourself from your contemporaries. You need a system that clearly separates you from the pack.

We all have heard the phrase "striving for excellence," but what do those words really mean? Do they mean that you should be motivated to achieve perfection every time you attempt something or that you have to be flawless in the execution of everything you do? Well, no. It means you should be the *best that you can be, each and every time*. When we look around us, it may seem that most people are not striving for excellence. Maybe that is because it is much easier to settle for mediocrity. Often it seems that many people's DNA tells them to do just what is required and not much more.

Look around, and you'll see evidence aplenty. Have you noticed the people who run a bit late for work but have their eye on the clock and are out the door a little early at the end of the day? Will those people volunteer for a tough project or will they avert their eyes from that challenge? Or, how many times have you heard, "We tried that before, and it didn't work," when someone brings up a new idea or offers a different approach to a problem? These are all examples of mediocrity in action.

On the other hand are those who are striving for perfection. They belong to a much smaller group, but sadly, the end result is frequently the same. They are often stuck in a rut and not moving steadily ahead. But wait, you say. Isn't perfection a good thing?

Not really. The truth is that perfection can rarely be achieved, and its pursuit often leads to inefficiency and wasted time precisely for that reason. Those who strive for perfection are often left frustrated or demotivated by the unappreciated reality that no matter how much effort they expend, they will never get to that perfect state.

"Excellence means doing your best today and
looking for ways to be better tomorrow."

Excellence is the sweet spot between mediocrity and perfection. It's doing more than what is required, and always working to improve, and it should be the focus of whatever pursuit you're after. The fact is that most of us can always do better than we are currently doing and can be better than we currently are. Constantly striving to improve ourselves is precisely how we can soar to new heights in our business and our life. Excellence means doing your best today and looking for ways to be better tomorrow. Relentless improvement should always be the objective. It's what your flight to excellence is all about.

Of course, it's easy to say, "Strive for excellence." It's like saying, "If you want to lose weight, eat less and exercise more." We all know that, yet millions of people have that knowledge, want to be slimmer, and just can't shed the weight. Most people need a process, a system, or a construct of some sort to help in achieving their goals. For the person who wants to lose weight, the solution might be a personal trainer, a group like Weight Watchers, or a great new book. There is no one perfect method. It's whatever works best for them. But the process they choose becomes the throttle that moves them forward toward accomplishing their objective.

The same concept holds true when striving for any type of excellence. Most people need both the motivation and a process to successfully move to a greater personal or professional level. The incentives can be many and different for every person: advancement in your company, building your own business, growing a healthy increase in the bottom line, or having better relationships with family and close friends. Once you decide where you want to go on your particular flight to excellence, you'll need a proven process that works for you.

I'm going to offer a process that has worked for me. It is a method I have shared with others, most recently in my speaking engagements but also throughout my professional life. The adherents to the process have obtained amazing results. Students having difficulty in pilot training have gone on to complete the training program near the top of the class. Entrepreneurs I have counseled have built successful businesses, and several executives I've coached have become CEOs. I call it the P4 System because the four key engines that power success all begin with the letter *P*, and it gives clear direction on how to achieve excellence in your life. It has worked to make me a multimillionaire and enabled me to literally pilot my way to success.

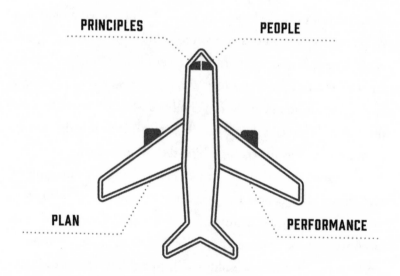

But let me be clear. I was not endowed with amazing gifts or incredible talents. Nor was I raised in an environment of privilege or advantage. Quite the contrary! I grew up as a young black kid in Orangeburg, South Carolina, when segregation was still the law of the land, at a time and in a place where the opportunities for a young African American male were limited and few. My mom and dad were teenage parents—sixteen and nineteen years old when they got married. I came along a year and a half later, and shortly thereafter, my dad was drafted into the army to go fight in the Korean War. It was clearly an inauspicious beginning for the Thompson family household.

Yet, despite this history, I have been blessed to live an interesting and fulfilling life. As the country began to go through a transformation due to the civil rights legislation of the mid-1960s and the leadership of Dr. Martin Luther King Jr. and others, I became very involved in the civil rights movement as a young teen. I was arrested and spent time in jail for demonstrating at the Orangeburg County Courthouse on August 3, 1965, when I was fourteen.

Later that fall, I joined eleven other African American students in integrating all-white Orangeburg High School and, for a time, was escorted to school by police each day. It was during this period that I began to unconsciously follow what would become my P4 System as I strove for excellence and success in what was a hostile new environment.

My four years at Orangeburg High were difficult and filled with daily challenges. But I also experienced daily victories, as the benefits of applying my steadily evolving P4 System began to take hold, and this young black kid saw human nature, attitudes, and behavior in my teachers and fellow students start to change. With resolve and growing confidence as the obstacles to success began to fall, I started to see the true potential of being in what was a unique and unusual situation. I began to envision possibilities that would have been unimaginable to my forefathers.

By my senior year, I had been fortunate to receive appointments to two of our nation's service academies, and the Air Force Academy was my eventual choice. To say that this profoundly changed my life would be a tremendous understatement. I later found out that I was the first African American from South Carolina to go to this prestigious Colorado school. Many members of my family were teachers, and although I had not yet given my future occupation serious thought, teaching seemed to be a natural consideration for me as well. But my appointment to the Air Force Academy was a life-changing paradigm shift. I could do more than teach in a classroom; I could literally reach for the sky.

Going to the Academy opened a world to this unsophisticated country boy that was previously unthinkable. I got to fly in fighter jets, learned to fly airplanes myself, and earned my skydiving wings. I traveled across the country and to different points across the globe—all during my cadet years while I was getting one of the best educations possible from one of the most prominent universities in the world. We were given leadership opportunities and had to make consequential decisions while many of our contemporaries in civilian universities were just trying to get through school without partying too hard.

The Academy was a very demanding place, with a tough four-year academic program, military training, and rigorous athletic requirements. It was a challenging journey, and I certainly had my ups and downs, as I was unprepared, in some ways, to compete on the national level with some of the best and the brightest our country had to offer. What bridged the gap was my focus on the P4 System. I survived: My class began with 1,406 cadets, but only 844 of us graduated after those arduous four years.

After graduating from the Academy and a short tour on the staff, I was off to jet pilot training in southern Georgia. Learning to fly a fighter-type Air Force jet was exciting, exhilarating, and demanding, yet the timing could not have been worse. The war in Vietnam was winding down, and the Air Force had more pilots than it needed. The end result was a program for us new trainees that was even more challenging than it would normally have been. We began the program with forty-eight pilot trainees, and a year later only twenty-four of us pinned on our new Air Force silver pilot's wings.

Once again, the P4 System provided the anchor that was the underpinning for my success. I was the only Academy graduate in my pilot training class and, as the "senior" second lieutenant, I was appointed section leader. Some of my fellow classmates assumed that being an Academy grad gave me a secret advantage that contributed to my achievement, and they sought my help. While I expect that spending four years at the Academy certainly gave me some imperceptible advantages, there were no direct benefits associated with getting through ground school and learning to fly the jet. I was, however, happy to share my approach to getting through the program, and my colleagues who adopted the P4 System also enjoyed similar success.

With my new silver wings, I was excited to go off and become an Air Force fighter pilot. Unfortunately, Uncle Sam had different plans. Ironically, because of our success in the training program, two of us were selected to immediately become instructor pilots and were sent to the Air Force's Pilot Instructor Training program in San Antonio, Texas. Even though this was a special honor, and I saluted smartly and accepted my fate, I was not ready to return to our Georgia base after completing training in Texas. I wanted to fly a different plane, enjoy new scenery, and have fewer mosquitoes to deal with. But for the time being, the needs of the Air Force took precedence.

While in pilot instructor training, I was offered the opportunity to go to Sacramento, California, to be a part of a new program that flew navigator trainees in fighter-type jets. I literally jumped at the chance. From southern Georgia to Northern California! The universe sometimes works in mysterious ways.

I enjoyed my best and last Air Force assignment in Sacramento. The flying was incomparable, the Sierra mountains were beautiful, and jetting over Lake Tahoe was absolutely stunning. Also, I was able to go to graduate school at night to work on a master's degree and then, after being bitten by the entrepreneurial bug, went off to law school to solidify my backup plan.

But two magazines, *Fortune* and *Entrepreneur*, changed my Air Force career plans: They opened my mind to the possibility of one day becoming a millionaire, which I had never considered before. With inflation soaring toward 15 percent and Congress debating whether to give the military a 3 or 4 percent pay raise, it was abundantly clear that the millionaire track didn't lie within the Air Force.

I began to look at other options, and the airline industry offered an attractive alternative. Delta Air Lines was the top carrier in the business, and they were gracious enough to offer me a job. I moved to Boston after my training with Delta to fly and to finish law school. After graduating and passing the bar, I opened a business and began to execute the next phase of my plan.

The business grew, which led to other financial opportunities—mostly winners but some losers, too. I also became interested in the political arena, and as time passed, I would serve in the administrations of four governors—two Democrats and two Republicans—overseeing the statewide aviation systems.

I sold my businesses and took an early retirement from Delta to begin a speaking and writing career, but fate intervened once again. The board of directors of the AOG (Association of Graduates), which represents the fifty thousand graduates from the Air Force Academy, offered me the opportunity to serve as the president and CEO. We put a broken house back in order, and our team enjoyed a stellar run growing our alumni chapters from thirty-one to eighty-five and increasing assets from $35 million to almost $60 million in just five years. We did it by establishing a clear vision and by getting and developing the right crew members. After all, a great organization comprises good people who have made the commitment to excellence and to do great things.

I have given these brief highlights of my background not to impress you or to pontificate on how great I am; it's really quite the opposite. As I shared with you earlier, I am no one special, and I wasn't born with the proverbial silver spoon in my mouth. But I have had the guidance of a method—the P4 System, which has worked exceedingly well for me during both good and very challenging times. It has been my guide when facing personal trials, financial troubles, and even the tribulations we all faced with COVID-19. It has been a top gun pilot for others who have employed it, and I truly believe it can work just as impressively for you.

So, are you ready to take the flight? Excellence is possible even if it is at times not an easy route. It requires both a decision on your part and the desire to be better than you currently are. And it will take discipline and determination when you inevitably fly through stretches of turbulent skies. But the possibilities are truly endless, and the rewards at your destination are more than you can imagine.

Can you do it? Of course you can. Since you're the master of your fate and the captain of your soul, it's your decision to make. We can't all be pilots, and all pilots can't fly jets. But those few who do, fly higher and faster than anyone else on earth. If you are ready for the journey, welcome aboard!

POWERING UP THE JET

"If a man does his best, what else is there?"

–GEORGE S. PATTON JR.,

American Army general, West Point Class of 1909

ON THEIR FIRST day at the United States Air Force Academy, the brand-new appointees, who are about to become basic cadets, begin their in-processing at Doolittle Hall, the alumni house of the Association of Graduates, better known as the AOG. Over the years, in-processing has become quite the event, with excited and delighted families accompanying the proud future cadets to the gorgeous Academy setting at the base of the Rampart Range of the Rocky Mountains.

It occurs on the last Thursday in June, when a radiant blue sky can be counted on and a towering Pikes Peak still wears its snowcap. The atmosphere is festive, with motivational greetings from the superintendent—the three-star general who runs the Academy—and the president and CEO of the AOG, a position I held for nine years. The families enjoy an informational fair inside the building while the new basic cadets are introduced to the history of Academy graduates on the adjoining Heritage Trail. After buying a plethora of Air Force T-shirts, hoodies, and other swag, the families bid their new basics good-bye as they climb aboard buses for the trip up the hill to the Cadet Area.

The first half of the ten-minute bus ride is quiet, as the new cadets take in the gorgeous scenery. Then all hell breaks loose as their "Flight to Excellence" begins. The two upper-class members of the training cadre shatter the silence with orders and instructions designed to send the clear message that mediocrity is over and will never be accepted again. As the bus pulls up to the Core Values Ramp in the Cadet Area, the new basics exit and are greeted by both the rest of the upper-class training cadre and the Air Force's core values. The brushed aluminum letters hang high and prominent over the wall: Integrity First, Service Before Self, Excellence in All We Do.

The new cadets spend what seems to be an eternity enduring shouted directions and "corrections" as it becomes clear that excellence is going to be the standard: excellence in posture and how they stand, excellence in remembering and repeating the required responses, and excellence in obeying each command. Any basics who are slow to adjust get some "extra attention" before they are all led up the Ramp by an upper-class cadet. Their Air Force Academy experience is about to begin.

Basic cadets at the Core Values Ramp on their first day at the United States Air Force Academy. Photo courtesy of the Association of Graduates | United States Air Force Academy.

EXCELLENCE IN MY DNA

Though it was physically tough, intellectually demanding, and mentally challenging, I adapted well to the Academy environment. Wearing my uniform correctly, keeping my room in order, and shining my shoes were not challenges for me. These military chores were extensions of how I had been taught to live my life back home in Orangeburg, South Carolina. My parents, Willie and Pearl, showed me what excellence was by how they lived their lives. My mother handled the finances in the home and ran a tight ship, all while being a sharp dresser and frugal with the limited funds they had. My dad would let me help wash the car, a used 1951 Chevy that he always kept sparkling clean. The subtle but clear messages conveyed that your appearance mattered and taking care of your possessions was an important task. Our home was small but tidy, and keeping my room neat and clean became a part of my DNA. I had regular chores and was expected to contribute to the family's improvement. Over time we began to live small but growing parts of the American Dream. I can remember when both of my parents graduated from the local college, South Carolina State. My mom graduated in 1956 when I was five years old, and my dad finished a year later, delayed by his service in the US Army. They would both go on to obtain advanced degrees, and that up close example of them working hard and using education as a stepping-stone became an indelible part of my experience.

Having two parents who were schoolteachers was both a blessing and a curse. Though I didn't appreciate it at the time, I was fortunate to have parents who demanded that I do my best and be the best I could be. Meeting those expectations sometimes meant passing on enjoyable school activities or giving up playtime with my neighborhood friends.

Perfection was never their objective for me; their aspiration was that I would give my all. And my parents were intuitive enough to understand the subtleties of the difference. The rule at home was that I could play with friends or participate in after-school activities as long as I maintained good grades in my courses. If my grades dropped, the restrictions kicked in. If I was playing a sport, for example, I had to come off the team.

In junior high, I was on our school basketball team and had made the starting five. I was also struggling with a system briefly introduced in the 1960s called new math. My dad was pretty good at math, but even he had trouble understanding the concepts when I went to him for help with my homework. When I got my report card, my math grade had slipped from a B– to a C+, and I knew the rule would require me to quit the team. When I showed my dad my report card, he said, "I see you are still battling with that math." My response was simply, "Yes, sir." He said, "Keep after it, and you'll eventually do OK." I expected him to reiterate the rule and tell me that I was off the team, but he didn't say anything else. The next day I didn't know whether I should stay for basketball practice or go home because of the rule. I decided it would be better to ask for forgiveness rather than permission, so I stayed for practice. When I got home, my father never said a word, and I continued to be on the team. Years later, as I reflected on that situation, I realized that my dad only wanted me to do my best, and because he knew I was putting in the time and effort, he was OK with relaxing the rule. Striving for excellence and doing my best was the goal, and in his eyes, I had met the standards.

INTEGRATING HIGH SCHOOL

While my upbringing at home prepared me well in many ways for my Academy experience, going to Orangeburg High School gave me mental toughness and prepared me for the psychological trials and tribulations that every cadet at a service academy has to endure. In fact, in some ways the Academy experience was easier because all my classmates and I were going through the same challenges as a team, and we formed a strong bond among us when we made it through a particularly tough stretch. But there were only twelve African Americans out of twelve hundred students at Orangeburg High, and the sense of isolation and vulnerability made a hostile situation even more intimidating.

There were two segregated high schools in my hometown: Orangeburg High (OHS), the "white" high school on the other side of town, and Wilkerson High School for the African American students, which was one block up and two blocks over from where I lived. Though it was right around the corner, Wilkerson was not my first choice for high school. I had gone to the black Catholic school in my hometown, and after graduating eighth grade I wanted to go to an all-boys' school, St. Emma's Military Academy in Virginia. I sent for the catalog but after seeing the costs, I quickly got the sense from my folks that it was going to be too expensive to send me there. I accepted that I would go to Wilkerson, which would have been just fine. It was close, my favorite aunt was on the faculty, and most of my neighborhood friends would be there as well. The passage of the Civil Rights Act in 1964 changed the landscape and unexpectedly gave me another option. Under a program called the Freedom of Choice plan, I decided to go to OHS.

It was a decision that my parents left to me. We certainly discussed it numerous times—the opportunity advantages and social disadvantages, other pros and cons, the true danger that might exist, and how the risks might be lessened. Alone with my thoughts, I vacillated and wavered back and forth. It would be easier going to Wilkerson, where I would be hanging out with my close buddies and be around other people I knew. It's very important when you are fourteen to be comfortable as a part of a familiar group.

But by helping to integrate OHS, I would be part of something significant and bigger than myself. I would be a tangible part of the civil rights movement—a frontline soldier in the battle against bigotry and prejudice. It was kind of weighty when I thought about it. But deep down, I knew it was essentially the right thing to do to help integrate this school, not only for our African American community but, though they didn't appreciate it at the time, for the white community as well. When I shared my decision with my parents, my mother looked me in the eyes and said, "William, if you are going to go over there, don't you shame us. It is going to be hard, but we still expect you to do the very best that you can do every day. And if you do that, you'll be just fine." So, with excellence as my charge, I became a part of the first class of African American students to spend all four years at OHS.

I'll never forget my first day of high school. I left home that morning and walked down to the end of the block to wait for the school bus. I was by myself because I was the only kid from my neighborhood who was going to OHS. As I stood there waiting, I could see several police cars off in the distance with their lights flashing, headed in my direction. My first thought was that there had been an accident somewhere up the road and the cops were headed to that scene. But with no sirens blaring, I thought maybe there was something more nefarious at play. My imagination began to run away, and I surmised that maybe it was a break-in or a robbery. That might explain their silent approach. Well, imagine my astonishment when this caravan of police cars and the school bus stopped right in front of me. This was my federal marshal and highway patrol escort for my first day of school.

I got on the bus, and we picked up a couple of other kids before heading over to OHS. As I sat there taking in the whole scene, I briefly thought that having your own police escort to go to school was actually pretty cool. But that feeling drained away when we reached the OHS parking lot. There to greet us was an angry mob with ax handles and baseball bats who rushed up and began to pound the side of the bus before the cops could move them back. They shouted obscenities and racial slurs and told us we didn't belong—that we should turn around and go back to our own school.

We got off the bus that day and walked into history. We marched between two lines of screaming humanity, being called names, shouted at, and spat upon. I admit that for a brief moment I wondered why I had chosen to do this and thought about getting back on the bus and going home. But we were there for the greater good. More importantly, the fear of embarrassment from not doing my best, and heeding my mom's advice to perform with excellence, was greater than the fear of what lay ahead. It was the first day of four of the most fascinating, challenging, and, in many ways, fulfilling years of my life.

Some folks find it surprising that I regarded those years as fulfilling and are amazed that I didn't take a sense of anger or resentment with me from the experience. In reality, I felt fortunate to have a pilot's window on human nature and to see firsthand how many of my white classmates, over time, began to change.

THE VALUE OF LUNCHROOM REAL ESTATE

In the beginning we were novelties, and there was a universal sense of how we were to be treated and how the white students were supposed to act. The running yarn was that they were not supposed to get too close to us, as the "black might rub off." One result was that when we walked down the corridors, the white students would dramatically jump to the side so as not to get too close. In most of my classes, there was an empty desk in front and back and on either side of me. And when I went to lunch and sat at a table that seated twenty-four, everyone else would get up and I would have twenty-three empty seats to myself. I found this particularly amusing, as the lunchroom was usually full and seats were hard to come by. Yet the white students would stand in the aisles and eat from their trays rather than join me at the table.

For several different reasons that coalesced over time, things began to slowly change. Common sense began to take hold in the lunchroom. I distinctly remember everyone getting up on cue when I sat down one day and then a girl reticently sitting back down while saying, "I won't be too close to him if I sit here on the end." A few of her friends hesitantly joined her, and that became the new norm—you could sit at the same table but not too close. Of course, the value of a lunch table seat was still at a premium, and in relatively short order the acceptable space between me and my white classmates began to shrink and became just a couple of seats. A little bit of integration was beginning to take place.

TACKLING PREJUDICE

I was the first black kid to go out for the football team, which involved a totally different dynamic. Initially, my fellow teammates attempted to play the same "separation" game that was in play up on campus. But the rules were different on the football field. My coach, Jack Miller, would have none of it. When one of the players didn't want to have a locker next to mine, Coach Miller told him to go find another sport to play, and that sent a shock wave through the room. The next player assigned a locker next to me had nothing to say.

There were other factors that made football different from the rest of the daily school experience. Of course, football is a contact sport with equal opportunity to hit and be hit. After a long day up on campus dealing with a variety of slights, annoyances, and indignations, I saw football practice as an opportunity to take out my frustrations with the circumstances that I had to deal with. Ironically, that opportunity for both my mental and physical "release" got me noticed by the coaches and I began to build both a reputation and respect among my fellow teammates as a hard-hitting player.

Football, like most sports, has a winner and a loser, and it feels so much better when your team wins the game. This was another important factor that distinguished the football experience from the interactions at the rest of the school. Having the common goal and purpose of winning, coupled with respect for what I brought to the fight, hastened my acceptance as a member of the team. During the early days of practice, I got the silent treatment from my teammates, which was par for the course at school. As time progressed, however, I would sporadically get a nod of approval or a "nice job" when I was involved in a good play. It wasn't long before I was talked to in the locker room or occasionally included in a conversation.

The South loves its football, and the top players earn a unique position, deserved or not, among the game's fans. Orangeburg, on its microscopic scale, was no different. The top players from our team also enjoyed a special status with many of the other students at school. Call it admiration, respect, or maybe just the fact that they were on the sports pages of our local paper, but it was clear to me that some of our players were "big men on campus." Other than observing this fact, I thought it was of no consequence to me until one day on campus when I walked by one of the star teammates, who said, "Hey, Willie," which caught me totally by surprise. He and others had spoken to me periodically in the gym or on the football field, but no one had ever spoken to me on campus. What was equally surprising was his response to the girl he was walking with when she asked, "You said hi to that [N-word]?"

He said, "Oh, Willie is a pretty good ole boy." A couple of days later, I happened to walk by the same girl who had been with the star when he had greeted me. She looked at me and nodded in acknowledgment, and I nodded back. Once again, on a small scale, integration was beginning to take place.

The situation with the star and his girlfriend rattled around in my brain for several days thereafter. I broke it down into its elementary parts. His acceptance of me on the football field had transferred to accepting me on campus, and that acceptance, witnessed by his girlfriend, had transferred to her. Admittedly, this overthinking analysis sounds a bit trite today, but it has to be viewed through the eyes of a fourteen-year-old in an intimidating and unfriendly environment who had just experienced a small glimmer of optimism.

The seed of a plan began to form. I decided that I would cautiously but deliberately begin to engage some of the other stars on the team. Of course, I would have to carefully feel them out, as there were many players on the team who didn't want me there but quietly acquiesced because of Coach Miller's stance. Yet I did begin to develop superficial relationships with several starting players, including the quarterback, and it got to the point that we were comfortable greeting each other at the beginning of practice or saying good night as we left the gym. Once that habit pattern was established, I took the "greeting" show "on the road" to the campus area. When I would pass one of my new "buddies" in the corridors or in the lunchroom, I would offer a quick greeting, and with few exceptions it was returned. There is no analytical data to support my feelings, but I firmly believe this is one of the reasons that I began to be marginally accepted or, more accurately, not be harassed as much by the other students.

BEYOND EXPECTATIONS

The football dynamic is easily understandable and initially gave me an advantage my other African American colleagues did not enjoy. As time passed, my status on the team began to grow, which was predictable to an extent. Yet the most unexpected, surprising, and notable attention I received at OHS didn't occur on the football field. It happened in BSCS Biology[1] class during the first semester of my sophomore year.

At the beginning of the semester in my homeroom class, I discovered that my previously submitted schedule had been drastically changed. Instead of the college prep track that I had signed up for, my schedule had been altered to take basic math and general science with a shop course thrown in for good measure. When I spoke to my homeroom teacher about it, she told me that the college prep track would be too difficult for me and she had changed my schedule to help me out. Quite honestly, I believed that she felt she was doing the right thing for me. She was actually a sweet, older, traditional lady, and I didn't attribute any maliciousness to her actions. I did, however, politely but firmly insist that my schedule be changed back to my original choices, which she reluctantly did.

The BSCS Biology course was in the college prep track and was offered at several different periods during the day. The class included both sophomore and junior students and was considered a pretty tough course. At some point during the semester, a standardized test was given to all students taking the course, and when we received the results, I felt pretty good with my performance. I had missed a few questions but was pleased overall with my score.

---

1   BSCS Science Learning is an independent nonprofit offering science education research and leadership programs and curriculums across the United States. BSCS.org.

What I did not know was that I had received the highest score of all students taking the course.

Word of that result spread through the school like wildfire. When I walked down the corridor to my classes, huddled students pointed at me and whispered. Still unaware of the total test results, I was oblivious to why I had suddenly become the center of so much attention and naturally assumed that it was something bad. I did eventually overhear a student who pointed to me say, "There's that smart [N-word]," but I had no context for his comment. It wasn't until I went to biology class the next day and Dr. Turner, the teacher, announced my standing in the overall results that I understood what had been happening.

Clearly, the expectations for my academic performance were extremely low. One of my classmates in that same class, who sat one desk over and one desk back, asked me how I was able to cheat so well. He told me that he watched me like a hawk, saw my test and quiz scores when they were returned to me, and just could not figure out how I was cheating. He had been taught to believe that all blacks were "dumb, shiftless, and lazy," so it never even occurred to him that I could actually perform. I quickly realized that this might be an opportunity to expand my sway beyond the football team by similarly, strategically targeting the honor-student crowd. Striving for excellence in the classroom could bring me even more respect than being a top jock. The seed of another plan began to form.

My career at OHS was, by most measures, successful. I received Honorable Mention All-American honors in football and Amateur Athletic Union recognition in track. On the academic front, I received a National Merit Commendation, appointments to two of our nation's service academies, and scholarships to several top schools. Most important, I got to see, up close and personal, the positive change in people's mindsets and attitudes as exposure and interaction counteracted the stereotypes that had been the foundation of their beliefs. I also discovered in a concrete way the tangible advantages of striving for excellence in the classroom and on the football field. Yes, I benefited directly from the athletic and academic effort. Even more important was the marginally more positive environment that it began to create for my other African American schoolmates and how it helped to change a hostile and adverse setting.

THE P4 SYSTEM

As my career progressed, I often reflected on the methods and strategies I had used to get through the OHS experience in a positive way. Those techniques, coupled with the values instilled in me by my mom and dad, formed the basis for a consistent approach, a steady and reliable routine for achieving my goals. Following the P4 System, and following this process has been the foundation for what I have been able to achieve in my professional life.

The P4 System: Principles, People,
Flight Plan, Performance

The four key components of the route to success all start with the letter *P*, ergo the P4 name. The components are as follows:

➢ PRINCIPLES

➢ PEOPLE

➢ A flight PLAN

➢ PERFORMANCE

These factors provide the power necessary to soar to amazing heights.

PRINCIPLES

The first and most important component is Principles. Without the proper moral foundation and ethical motivation, any subsequent accomplishment is transitory at best and won't stand the scrutiny of enduring success. Your principles are critically important because they define your life. They are the values that determine the things you do and dictate the choices you make. It is crucial that your principles are integrity-based if you are to ultimately achieve excellence and enjoy long-term sustained success.

PEOPLE

With a principled foundation in place, you will now need to surround yourself with the right People and respect and take care of the people you lead. Having the right flight crew—people who are ethical, intelligent, positive thinking, and share your vision—is critically important both to achieving the immediate mission and helping you attain your longer-term goals. As the captain of your own destiny, you're responsible for looking for and wisely choosing your colleagues, followers, and friends. You may find that the people who currently surround you don't fit these criteria, which may lead to some difficult choices. But you will need to accept that as you grow and advance, some of your old crew may have to be left behind. You'll need to identify "influencers" like I did at Orangeburg High, who can help you move your agenda forward, and seek out mentors for insight and guidance to help you soar.

A FLIGHT PLAN

The third component of the P4 System is a flight Plan. That great philosopher Yogi Berra once said, "If you don't know where you are going, you'll end up someplace else." And he was right!

Most of us, at a basic level, understand the importance of planning, and we do it often in a host of everyday ways. We'll plan to go to the grocery store, often with a list of the things we want to buy. We'll plan a trip and take care of all the things we need to do: get a plane ticket, notify our friends or relatives when we'll arrive, pack all the items we need to take with us, and get to the airport on time.

But most people don't bring these simple planning skills to the critical aspects of their professional, personal, or financial lives. Do you know where you want to be in two or five years and what you'll need to do to get there? Do you have it written out in a definitive way, with the steps you'll need to accomplish to arrive on time? The truth is, most people don't have a written plan with specific goals.

What percentages of people do? There are the often-cited Harvard and Yale studies that assert that only 3 percent of people had written down their goals, but that 3 percent had, on average, ten times the wealth of those who didn't.

Though popularized by self-help gurus like Brian Tracy and Tony Robbins, these studies were never actually conducted. There is, however, a recent study by Dr. Gail Matthews of Dominican University of California and Steven Kraus of Harvard to determine the impact of goal setting. It turns out the results often touted in the mythical studies are actually true. People who have flown to great levels of success have begun the journey with a well-developed flight Plan.

PERFORMANCE

The final component of the P4 System is Performance. While all of the prior components are critically important, nothing will happen until you perform. As the captain, you have to actually fly the jet.

═══

Let's expand on the flight analogy and review where we currently are. You understand the Principles of flight. You have a talented group of People: a brilliant copilot, an able flight crew, and a plane-load of wonderful passengers. You have completed a great flight Plan. Without Performance, however, the plane goes nowhere. You, the captain, have to take action to execute the Flight to Excellence. You'll need to push up the power, steer the jet down the runway, pull back on the controls, and get that giant metal bird up in the sky. Once you have performed and gotten the plane airborne, you'll be able to pilot that jet to incredible altitudes and travel great distances. Likewise, achieving great heights and traveling far in life requires Performance on your part. Action is the jet engine that gives you the power to propel yourself toward achieving your goals.

Of course, it is human nature to procrastinate, and there are a number of reasons why we do: lack of confidence, laziness, being overwhelmed, or just plain FEAR (Failure of Excellence, Achievement, and Rewards). Striving for excellence will give you the tools to overcome inaction and enable you to achieve unimaginable success.

The P4 System has been my constant practice and a dependable copilot along my personal flight to success. P4 helped me to become an Air Force pilot and, eventually, an international check captain with Delta Air Lines. It assisted me in becoming a lawyer and millionaire entrepreneur. P4 aided and supported me in serving four governors on both sides of the aisle, to successfully oversee state agencies. And P4 provided the tools that enabled me to lead a major association to unbelievable heights. It has also helped countless others, and my bet is that it can help you too. So, come join me in the cockpit, and let's strap in. I'll be your copilot on this incredible journey, to help you get airborne and fly to remarkable heights. And I promise a most exciting and rewarding flight.

= PART I =
PRINCIPLES

*"A people that values its privileges above
its principles soon loses both."*

—DWIGHT DAVID EISENHOWER,
thirty-fourth president of the United States,
West Point Class of 1915

THE POWER OF PRINCIPLES

> *"Great ambition is the passion of a great character. Those endowed with it may per-form very good or very bad acts. All depends on the principles which direct them."*
>
> —NAPOLEON BONAPARTE,
> French emperor and military commander

I WAS SITTING alone in the cockpit of a Delta Boeing 767 jumbo jet at LaGuardia Airport in New York City, programming the flight computers for the trip down to Fort Lauderdale, Florida. The flight attendant in charge popped in and asked if I had time to chat with an anxious passenger who had just boarded the flight. She was a well-dressed, professional woman who was deathly afraid of flying, and the attendant hoped that talking to the captain might help ease her fears. I invited her in and had her sit in the other pilot's seat, while noticing that she was clearly under a lot of stress.

She immediately began to explain that she was terrified of flying and had no idea of how an airplane flew. What was happening in the cockpit when the jet was in the air was a total mystery to her, and she just knew that when we went through turbulence, the wings were likely to fall off the plane.

I gave her a big, broad smile that put her a little bit more at ease and began to explain, in lay terms, the basic principles of how an airplane flies. I showed her our programmed route of flight to Fort Lauderdale, the major cities we would be flying over along the way, and the weather briefing that had been prepared for our flight. After pulling out my phone, I showed her online pictures of some of the many stress tests that airline manufacturers conduct on their planes and how flexible the wings actually are.

She asked me some questions about flying in general and specifically about our trip, and as she began to develop a better understanding of the principles of flight and got more information about what we were going to do, she became less apprehensive about her perceived impending catastrophe. At the very least, she was clear on the fact that the wings were never going to fall off because of any rough air on the way down south.

During the flight, as we turned to leave the mainland around North Carolina and headed out over the ocean, we did encounter some turbulence, and I couldn't help but wonder how she was handling things in back. But later during the trip, she sent up a note to say that she was doing just fine. At the arrival gate in Florida, as she left the airplane she told us that it was the best flight, by far, that she had ever had.

PRINCIPLES—UNDERSTANDING THE RULES

The initial conversation with that Florida passenger and her subsequent experience on the flight clearly illustrate the power of the first element of the P4 System. Knowing the principles associated with your endeavors is fundamental to understanding what is going on in general and—more specifically—how it may affect you. Also, understanding principles is often the key, in a broader context, to maximizing opportunities or avoiding significant risk. As the saying goes, "You can't win the game if you don't understand the rules." Principles are akin to rules. Sadly, many folks never comprehend this simple notion and go through life either uninformed, living in a haze of ignorance, or sometimes, like the Florida traveler, even existing in a state of outright fear.

Airline travel is a good illustration of this indisputable truth. Almost everyone has seen an airplane, and many people have flown on one. Numerous individuals find the experience truly wondrous, but a substantial number of people are uneasy at best, and a significant minority is completely terrified of being in the air. Since very few folks actually know how an airplane flies, they are unaware of the underlying principles of flight that ensure that it flies every time.

Fundamental principles govern almost every aspect of our lives. Principles concerning proper diet and exercise affect our overall health and determine how we look and feel. Principles of decency, respect, and how we interact with people affect our relationships with others and determine how we are perceived. Principles regarding spending habits, savings, and investing determine where and how we live and how much wealth we will amass. Likewise, just as with flying and other aspects of life, there are underlying principles of excellence that, when consistently applied, will ultimately lead to a meaningful measure of achievement and success.

Most of us greatly admire those who have achieved excellence in their various pursuits. Michael Jordan is considered to be the greatest basketball player ever to have played the game, and whether you love or hate the New England Patriots, you have to give Tom Brady his due as being the GOAT, the greatest of all time, as the best quarterback in NFL history.

We have great respect for any students who achieve prodigious academic excellence and go on to one of the nation's top universities like Stanford, MIT, the Ivy League schools, or one of our nation's military service academies. We have much esteem for successful businesspeople like Jeff Bezos of Amazon and Elon Musk of Tesla and SpaceX for their vision, ingenuity, and resourcefulness. In the arts, who would argue that Meryl Streep, with three Oscars and twenty-one nominations, isn't the best actor of our time? And one of my favorite groups of greatly admired people are our nation's astronauts, who have traveled literally out of this world—and some all the way to the moon.

While most folks recognize and respect the distinction these people and others like them have achieved, many assume that they were born with special gifts and unique talents and were destined for excellence from the beginning. But the overwhelming majority of them would tell you that was not the case. What you *would* find, however, is that they shared very similar principles. Most people who have chosen to live by specific principles have universally achieved excellence in their chosen fields and have enjoyed tremendous success.

The key point here is that we can all choose to strive for excellence. The principles, characteristics, and beliefs that successful people employ are elements that practically anyone can adopt. We can all be better than we currently are. And this presents a fantastic opportunity for those who understand this salient fact and who make a conscious decision to strive for excellence in their lives.

Unfortunately, it can often feel as if mediocrity has become the order of the day. Our public school system is a case in point. Despite our government spending more on education than most of the world's other developed nations, our children's academic performance is below average when compared to our peers in other countries. Granted, the issues facing some of our schools are many and complex. Yet excellence in our K–12 public school systems remains an elusive goal.

Equally discouraging is the lack of excellence sometimes seen in businesses. All too frequently, we get the feeling that the customer is an afterthought, if we're considered at all. When corporate leaders worship at the altar of short-term profits, the result can be a poor customer experience. Have you ever experienced an automated answering system that caught you up in menu-loop hell? And it's the exception to the rule when we obtain a service appointment at a predetermined, stated time. The norm is that we waste up to half a day waiting during a four-hour window in which the service was promised to take place. And more often than not, you had better not have a problem that falls outside some companies' standard protocols. If it takes any imagination to resolve the issue, the refrain is likely to be "I'm sorry, we can't help you," at least not without a price increase or some other charge. Just try to change your flight reservation for the same fare.

We have an overcrowded legal system where several states have declared "judicial emergencies." This results in long waits for a trial, and therefore, justice is delayed. Our increasingly costly health-care system is hostage to a dysfunctional political structure where even the party in power's members can't agree among themselves on how to reach a commonsense solution. Should we have "Medicare for all" or a system that has a government option to supplement employer coverage? Or do we "repeal and replace" the current system, even when there is no current plan offered to trade?

Unfortunately, these are just a few examples where the citizen/customer should be the focus of service but is often not. Yet they all present tremendous opportunities to effect significant change by a laser-like focus on the principles of excellence.

PRINCIPLES

The word *principle* is a homograph, which is a word that is spelled one way but has different meanings. On the one hand, a principle can be defined as "a general law or fundamental rule about how something works," as we discussed regarding how an airplane flies. But principle also means "a guiding sense of the obligations of right conduct; an ethical standard that someone believes in; a set of values."

PRINCIPLES—CORE VALUES

Having the proper values is crucial to servant leadership and to achieving excellence in life. Your values are critically important because they define who you are, the things that are important to you, and what you will ultimately do in any given situation. Without a strong underpinning of ethical and moral values buttressed by integrity at the core, the temptation to do what is expedient, profitable, or personally advantageous—even when corrupt—can be overwhelming. An unethical approach may sometimes lead to short-term gain, but it is ultimately and always a losing strategy.

A host of well-known examples proves that fact. In the corporate arena, Ken Lay and Jeff Skilling of Enron shame and Bernie Ebbers and Scott Sullivan who at WorldCom oversaw the largest bankruptcy in US history are instructive. And who can forget Bernie Madoff, the financier who bilked thousands of people out of billions of dollars in the largest Ponzi scheme ever? They all, for a while, lived glamorous lives and made millions of dollars but were ultimately convicted of multiple crimes and, with the exception of Lay, who died of a heart attack while awaiting sentencing, have all gone to jail. The connection between bankrupt principles and bankrupt companies appears to be clear.

In recent times, skewed values concerning sexual conduct have led to very public and difficult revelations for a number of people in high-profile and powerful positions. In the entertainment sector, Harvey Weinstein, Kevin Spacey, and Bill Cosby lead a growing list of celebrities who have been charged with inappropriate and even criminal sexual activity. National political figures like Senator Al Franken, Judge Roy Moore, and even President Donald Trump have all been exposed in salacious situations of their own creation.

There is also a host of notorious historical examples. Adolf Hitler, Joseph Stalin, Idi Amin, and Saddam Hussein all led nations and attained great power and wealth, and their portraits were ubiquitous throughout their countries. But how do we view them today? They are remembered as pariahs of history, their names synonymous with infamy and disgrace.

Compare those examples with some of the most admired people in history. Dr. Martin Luther King Jr. stood for the principles of equal justice for all and nonviolent activism to achieve that goal. He was awarded the Nobel Peace Prize for his steadfast adherence to those principles. He is the only African American to have a national holiday named in his honor, and his statue on the National Mall in Washington, D.C., is a testament to his principles.

Senator John McCain, a Naval Academy graduate and Navy pilot, spent over five years as a POW in North Vietnam. Although he endured unspeakable torture and other hardships, his fundamental ethical principles enabled him to resist our country's enemy and to "return home with honor." After retirement from the Navy as a captain, he went on to serve two terms in the US House of Representatives and was elected US senator from Arizona for five consecutive terms. He was the Republican nominee for president in 2008, and though he lost to Barack Obama, he still enjoyed strong bipartisan respect in Congress and among the American public at large. He died in 2018 and lay in state in the Capitol, an honor reserved for the country's most revered figures.

President Nelson Mandela of South Africa fought against the evils of apartheid and spent twenty-seven years in prison for his principles. He was offered his freedom on several occasions on the condition that he renounce those principles, but being a man of integrity, he refused to do so. Mandela was eventually freed, won the Nobel Peace Prize in 1993 for his work on reconciliation between blacks and whites in South Africa, and in 1994 became the country's first freely elected democratic president.

"Principles are not something you have to think about, because they are your being."

It's important to remember that we can be very successful by playing within ethical rules and still enjoy a superior level of achievement that will endure. The key is to have high personal standards coupled with the proper values. Your principles should embody the things you do, and the things you do should represent the principles you live by. Principles are not something you have to think about, because they are your being. Ultimately, your principles have to be the foundation and infrastructure of your life.

━━━━━━

It's prudent to self-evaluate periodically to check the congruency of your stated values and your actual actions. Are your principles based on integrity and geared to help you get the most out of life? Are your values focused to empower you to enjoy the greatest possible personal growth, to be the best you can be across the board, to live a life of excellence?

If your answer is no, then what needs to change? Could it be your relationships or your friends? It may be the conditions of your work environment or even the very nature of your job. Could it be your social activities or the lack thereof? You may even come to the conclusion that at this point, you need a total lifestyle change. The indisputable fact is that you design your life by the values you create and adopt, and excellence in your principles is fundamental to achieving and sustaining high levels of admiration, respect, and success.

Now that our flight visibility is clear on the importance and value of having the right principles, let's dig deeper into integrity, the most important principle of all.

INTEGRITY FIRST

*"Any individual or business that is completely
honest in all its dealings is likely to succeed."*

—C. E. WOOLMAN,
founder of Delta Airlines

INTEGRITY

It is certainly no mistake that Integrity is the first of the Air Force's three core values, because integrity is the foundation upon which the other two core values, Service and Excellence, are built. By its very definition, integrity requires adherence to moral and ethical principles, compels soundness of character, and obliges honesty and truthfulness in your actions. Integrity governs your reputation and determines how people perceive and react to you. It determines whether people will trust you, respect you, and believe in you. Having integrity is critically important because it defines your values and is the essence of who you are, and as the captain, these qualities are critical if you are to successfully lead your flight crew.

These values were infused in me by my mom and dad and were constantly reinforced during my four years at the Air Force Academy. Yet we are all human, and there will be times when staying true to these values will be challenging. I've learned from experience that being a person of integrity is always the better choice.

CHANGING PLANES

I was on cloud nine, living the dream! It was hard to believe that I was really here. As I looked around the tastefully appointed Delta corporate reception area, I was surprised to see that there were only a few other people in the room, and a couple of them appeared to be in their early twenties. *We are probably not here for the same job*, I quickly surmised, and after surveying the group more closely, I came to the conclusion that maybe only one other person in the room might be there for the same reason that I was.

Northern California was my home at the time. I was a captain in the Air Force, flying as an instructor pilot in the Cessna T-37 jet trainer at Mather Air Force Base in Sacramento. This two-engine jet was used to train new Air Force pilots, but at Mather, we had a special mission to train Air Force navigators. My tour at Mather and my initial service obligation to the Air Force were both coming to an end. I could continue to serve if I desired to, but I had paid back my time to Uncle Sam for putting me through the Academy on the taxpayers' dime.

I had recently received my new assignment to Edwards Air Force Base in Southern California, where my new flying job was to be in the Cessna A-37 attack fighter, the souped-up, fully equipped version of the trainer jet I had been flying. Though it had a big gun and carried more bombs, missiles, and rockets, it was still a Cessna 37, and I was looking to do (fly) something different. So here I was, down in Atlanta, Georgia, where in late spring, the weather was already getting hot and muggy.

The timing of my trip was fortuitous. At a time when the airline industry was in a downturn and hundreds of pilots from other major carriers were in furlough status (another way of saying laid off), I had managed to get a much sought-after interview for a pilot's job with Delta Air Lines.

Delta had not been my first choice when I decided to consider leaving the Air Force for the commercial aviation business. I was thoroughly enjoying Northern California and all it had to offer. Wine country, with the vineyards of Napa and Sonoma Valleys, was only forty-five minutes down Interstate 80, and the world-class casinos, top-tier entertainment, and skiing at Lake Tahoe were just a beautiful mountain drive away to the east. Though Delta had a stellar reputation in the airline business, it didn't have a West Coast base at the time, and as a result, it was not on my list of companies to pursue.

THE IMPOSSIBLE DREAM

There was, however, a common, good-humored quip among some of my fellow Air Force pilots at Mather: "Every pilot wants to be an airline pilot, and every airline pilot wants to be a Delta pilot." I had heard this adage several times, but being from the southeast and fully enjoying the California experience, I never gave Delta much thought. As the airline option became a more serious consideration, I decided it was in my best interest to actually determine what made Delta a great company and why this saying was a part of the pilot lore.

There was no Google back then, so I had to truck off to the local library to do the required research, and it didn't take long for me to understand the true story behind this genial axiom. It turns out that Delta was the most profitable airline in the history of aviation and had had thirty-five consecutive years of profit. Its pilots were the highest paid in the industry and, most notably, Delta had never furloughed its cockpit crews. Even during the economic downturn that ended in 1975, Delta had kept all of its pilots on the payroll, though junior pilots who weren't needed for flying were reassigned to other jobs in the company. The corporation considered all of the employees to be a part of the "Delta Family," and management's actions were true to those words.

Being a pragmatic person and fully appreciating the value of stable, long-term employment, I quickly came to the realization that enjoying the California lifestyle was secondary to working for the right company. Becoming an airline pilot was now my vision, and flying for Delta became the goal.

I have long enjoyed the classic song recorded by Andy Williams, "The Impossible Dream," and through my research, it quickly became apparent that just getting an interview with Delta would fit that definition to a "T" (pun intended). I learned that even in the best of times, Delta was very selective about who was invited to come to Atlanta, and the airline industry was now mired in a very troubled economic stretch.

Friends of mine and friends of friends who had gotten interviews with American Airlines, Eastern, or United couldn't get their foot in the door at Delta. A few who had even gotten interviews and were subsequently rejected by Delta had gone on to enjoy employment with some of those same respected carriers. Delta's fastidious approach to hiring its pilots, coupled with the state of the industry at that time, caused many colleagues to tell me I was wasting my time. Nonetheless, as I began my quest for getting an interview with a commercial airline, Delta had become for me—in the lyrics of that classic song—"the unreachable star."

GETTING TO ATLANTA: APPLYING THE P4 ELEMENTS

Like numerous other times before in my life, I began to apply the elements of the P4 System to accomplish my new and extraordinary goal. I developed a laser-like *focus* on getting invited to Atlanta for an interview. And—notwithstanding the economic environment and what little I had been able to learn about Delta's corporate culture—I deeply *believed* that I could impress the powers that were to invite me to Atlanta for a look-see. If I could get to Atlanta, I believed that I could get the job.

> *"I began to apply the elements of the*
> *P4 System to accomplish my new and*
> *extraordinary goal."*

As I began to put together my *flight plan* to become a Delta pilot, the irony of the situation was palpable. Initially, the California lifestyle had been my principal focus, and Delta hadn't even made my short list. But then, my values had totally shifted, and flying for Delta was my goal. I had come to realize that in the airline business, Delta represented excellence, and that was where I wanted to be.

Making optimum use of the *people* component of P4 was going to be crucial in achieving my goal. Through my Air Force Academy network, I was able to find a fellow graduate who was currently flying for Delta, and he provided me with key information about the company. Additional research got me the names of Delta's senior management, including Captain Harry Alger, chief pilot/vice president, flight operations; and Frank Rox, senior vice president for flight operations. As I discovered specific aspects of their bios that were similar to mine, I believed I could reference those commonalities to establish a connection.

Captain Alger had been an Air Force pilot who had served for six years, before separating to accept employment with Delta. Frank Rox was a fighter pilot during World War II, and after the war he had become a successful corporate lawyer. He eventually became Delta's vice president of law and public affairs before being promoted to his current position. I finished taking stock of our similarities and, as I have been known to say, "The seed of a plan began to form."

In the no-online world of 1980, I wrote and mailed a letter to Delta and requested two pilot applications. I completed them both and sent one back to the company through the normal flight operations and personnel route, and sent the other application with a cover letter to Frank Rox.

In the letter, I congratulated Mr. Rox and Delta for their consistent and enviable track record of profits and the company's reputation for giving outstanding service to its passengers. I also gave special mention to how Delta treated its employees or "family members"—treatment that was a rarity in the airline business. I shared my background as a fighter-type instructor pilot, mentioned my current enrollment in law school, and noted the similarities of our backgrounds in both those regards. I concluded the letter with an acknowledgment that although the aviation business was then going through some troubled times, Delta represented excellence to me and was the only airline that I wanted to fly for. I politely asked if he would keep my application on file for future reference when Delta started hiring pilots again.

I never received a response letter from Frank Rox but got something that was even more valuable: a phone call from Delta's employment office inviting me to Atlanta for an interview. The representative made it clear that Delta was not currently hiring pilots and didn't know when they would start hiring again. She told me they were only inviting in a few select applicants and would be pleased to have me come down for a conversation. So there I was, sitting in that tastefully appointed Delta reception area in the summer of 1980.

THE KIND OF PERSON YOU ARE

After some pleasant banter with the receptionist, I was shown back to the office of the director of pilot hiring, who was an institution in personnel at Delta and had interviewed hundreds of pilots over the years. The quintessential southern gentleman from Tennessee, Art could have been Colonel Sanders's brother, with a like mane of thick white hair. He graciously invited me to sit in a chair across from his desk. After I sat down, I began to take out my Air Force flight records and other supporting documentation and handed them to him. He took them and put them aside on his desk and started what I considered to be an introductory conversation to break the ice before the start of the interview.

He told me a bit about himself—where he was from and how long he had worked at Delta. He asked about my hometown of Orangeburg, South Carolina, a city that he knew. We talked about my family, and he asked me to share some of my experiences growing up in a small southern town. Then we talked about Delta and its southern roots, and he emphasized that Delta's success was due in great part to its conservative values.

The conversation was comfortable and flowing easily, and all the while, I waited for the official interview to begin. I had come prepared and was eager to talk about my flying record, my aviation skills, and Air Force experiences, and I wanted to explain how they would benefit Delta. Up to that point, we had just been talking about life in general and had yet to broach any of the subjects I felt so strongly about.

I finally asked him if he was going to inspect my flight records or ask me about my Air Force career. His response was just as casual as our conversation had been—and equally surprising. He said, "We know you can fly an airplane. You wouldn't be here if you couldn't. I want to find out what kind of person you are."

Well, any anxiety or apprehension that I may have had about the "official" interview instantly dissipated as we continued to have a quite enjoyable conversation. That is—until he asked me a couple of questions that were probably illegal at the time (and would certainly be unlawful today) that caught me totally off guard. He asked if I was a very religious man.

I thought back about my religion. I had grown up going to Catholic schools and was the first in my family to convert to Catholicism from the AME (African Methodist Episcopal) church that my parents attended. I had begun to lobby my parents to let me become a Catholic early in my grade school years, but my dad said I was too young to make that decision. We agreed that I would be allowed to choose my religion when I turned ten and was in the fifth grade.

To be honest, my enthusiasm to convert was totally practical: The Sunday service in the AME church lasted over two and a half hours, while Catholic Mass was over in about an hour. Additionally, most of my buddies at school were altar boys, and I wanted to be one too. The perks for those who served early-morning weekday Mass at school were hot chocolate and cinnamon rolls prepared by the nuns in the school cafeteria, and that was all the incentive I needed for both converting and getting up early!

My mom and younger sisters eventually converted as well, and I was a dedicated Catholic during high school and the early years of my time as a cadet at the Academy. My devotion and commitment began to wane during my later cadet tenure and my active-duty years in the Air Force. While I still went to Mass occasionally, I could not in good faith profess to be a very religious man.

So here it was: an ethical dilemma staring me in the face. I had gotten this precious interview at Delta, the model of excellence in the airline industry, at a time when they weren't even hiring pilots. I was having a fantastic "non-interview" with Art, who I was getting along marvelously with. He had underscored the fact that Delta was a conservative southern airline, and anyone who knows the South knows that church is a big part of the culture. I assumed that he was a religious man because he asked the question. What should I say? Should I lie to fit my perception of the model Delta pilot?

I was in law school at the time, and without appearing to hesitate too long, I quickly dug deep to bring my legal training to bear. My response was, "Yes, I do believe in God," hoping that answer would deflect any further questions along those lines. But it was not to be. The follow-up question was even more devastating. He asked point-blank, "Do you go to church every Sunday?"

I was caught with no place to go! As an Air Force Academy graduate, I had come from an institution with a strict honor code. Honesty and integrity were the foundation of how we operated in the Air Force. Most important, my parents had drummed into me from early childhood, "Always tell the truth."

But this was my big chance to become an airline pilot and with DELTA! It seemed my future aviation career was on the line. *If I tell the truth*, I thought, *my chances of getting a job with Delta are gone! Done! Over! Kaput!*

It's tough to appreciate the real difficulty of living your principles until the stakes are equally high.

LIVING YOUR PRINCIPLES

I sat there, sadly coming to the realization that flying for Delta was not to be. Though the temptation to lie was extremely strong, I could not in good conscience tell Art that I went to church every Sunday. Fudging just a bit to ease the sting, but resigned to telling the truth, I said, "I go to church when I can [that was the fudge], but no, I don't go to church every Sunday."

I was at once deflated, depressed, and dejected. I waited for the words I fully expected to hear, anticipating something on the order of "'T,' I like you, but we don't think you'll be a good fit with us at Delta, because we want pilots who have a strong relationship with God and who make it a point to go and worship every Sunday."

I began to feel impatient before he spoke again. I just wanted him to get it over with. I was thinking that this entire trip and interview had been a waste of time.

He said, "'T,' I'm glad to hear that you don't need to go to church every Sunday. We are an airline, and we fly 365 days of the year. Our pilots have to fly on Sundays. We wouldn't want to hire someone and potentially interfere with their strong religious beliefs."

I sat there—in shocked disbelief! That was certainly not the response I expected to hear. My immediate thought was how glad I was that I had told the truth, closely followed by wondering if this had been a test to see if I would lie to try to get a job. Art offered no additional information, and I asked no further questions. Two months later, I was in the August 1980 class of new-hire pilots, after Delta announced it would hire more than three hundred pilots between August and February of 1981. Having integrity and being true to my principles had won the day for me.

ATTITUDE CONTROLS YOUR ALTITUDE

> *"Think positively and masterfully, with confidence and faith, and life becomes more secure, more fraught with action, richer in experience and achievement."*
>
> **—EDDIE RICKENBACKER,**
> American fighter ace and
> Medal of Honor recipient

IT WAS ALMOST two o'clock, and as I sat at my desk, the familiar fear began to grip me. That all-too-well-known, uncomfortable heat was spreading through my body, and perspiration was starting to drip under my arms. I was glad that I had worn a sweater that day so no one would notice. I hoped again—as I had for each of the past several days—that they wouldn't be there waiting, and I could just make it to my next class safe and sound.

I was in my freshman year at Orangeburg High, and the feelings of tension from having several African American kids at what had been a segregated school in South Carolina were still quite high. To lessen the probabilities of and opportunities for conflict, I had developed a routine for getting around the campus as inconspicuously as a black kid in an all-white environment could.

Being in class was a bit of a haven, as there was adult supervision, but getting from class to class was like going out into the battlefield—you never knew when a sniper might attack. The main corridors of the school brought the greatest opportunity for a skirmish. With lots of students moving en masse, there was a higher likelihood that some kid would want to show off and try to impress his buddies by doing something stupid. My modus operandi was to take the corridors less traveled—fewer people and chances for trouble.

My strategy had been successful—for a brief while. One day, though, as I rounded the corner of the back corridor en route to sixth-period English class, there they were: my two new nemeses. The tall, lanky kid was leaning on the red pole that supported the overhead covering of the breezeway, and the other one, short and stocky, stood next to him with his hands on his hips. They reminded me of the old comic strip characters Mutt and Jeff, but I quickly learned that their actions were no joke.

As I approached them, they began what had become a routine for me—certain kids calling me racist names. In my short experience with integration, I had quickly learned to expect the usual language from some of my schoolmates and had become adept at mentally blocking it out. But this time things were different.

Mutt and Jeff positioned themselves on either side of me. As they walked along beside me, they shouted and threatened to seriously hurt me—even take my life. "A pine box would be too good for you!" the short one screamed. "We're going to send you home in a body bag."

With the adrenaline flowing, I figured I could take either one of them on, but the two-to-one odds had me concerned. I hastily put together a plan of defense and counterattack if they moved to follow up on their threats, all the while looking and walking straight ahead, pretending to ignore them.

They eventually began to fall back as I kept moving steadily forward. When they finally walked away in a different direction, a wave of relief engulfed me. I had averted disaster and dodged a cannonball.

My relief was short-lived—twenty-four hours, to be exact. As I rounded the corner the next day, they were there in that same spot by the red pole, and the vitriol began when I got close. They didn't walk beside me this time. They stayed by the pole, all the while shouting the same taunts until I was well away. They were there the next day, the day after, and the day after that. I was living my own version of *Groundhog Day*, and the now famous movie was still twenty-eight years away.

After five days of this bigoted harangue but with no other physical action on their part, I came to the realization that these guys were all talk. They had had ample opportunity to "put up" but were obviously content to just yell and scream. My fear had greatly waned, having been replaced by anger and disgust—and for a time, I seriously considered a plan to take them both on.

Several more days of the chorus followed, and I realized that getting into a scuffle with them was not a viable option. It wasn't worth the effort I would have to expend or the trouble I was sure to get into. Besides, my anger had slowly but measurably subsided. I was becoming indifferent to their insults and just ignored them as I walked on by.

On day twelve as I rounded the corner, I saw them in the distance sprinting full tilt to get to their usual spot. For some reason they were running late and were hustling to get to the red pole on time. In their rush, the short guy, the "Jeff" of the pair, tripped and went down hard but never missed a beat. He rolled over, jumped up, and brushed himself off, and then he limped a bit as he shuffled over to their spot. The whole episode was sidesplittingly funny, and I couldn't help but laugh. I thought to myself, *These guys are really a hilarious pair. I don't have a problem: I have a comedy show!* From that day on, I saw them as a couple of buffoons.

When I rounded the corner after that, I looked at them, chuckled, and even greeted them sometimes. At the end of week three, as I turned the corner and made my way toward the red pole, "Jeff" walked toward me and said, "Time-out. Can we call a truce?" I thought to myself, *You're the ones causing the problems,* but I said out loud, "Yeah, we can do that." Then he said, "Can I ask you a question?" And I said, "Go ahead. Shoot."

He asked, "How can you be such a coward and have such a yellow streak down your back? You take all this stuff that we have been giving you, and you never stand up and defend yourself. All you do is laugh and walk on by."

His question caught me off guard, and I had to think for a moment before answering. I finally replied, "I'm not a coward, because even though I know you guys are here waiting for me every day, I always come this way. And I laugh because I think what you guys are doing is funny. You are wasting your time rushing to be here on time and thinking that you're giving me a hard time. But you're not. I'm spending my time going to my next class so I can get an education, which is what I came here to do."

He didn't say anything, but a strange and puzzled look came over his face. It was an expression that I couldn't interpret at the time. But as I made my way the following Monday, Mutt and Jeff were gone, and I never saw them there again.

Some years later, I was talking to a friend and sharing some of my experiences at Orangeburg High. One of the stories I told her was the one that I have just shared. Shortly afterward, as I reflected on those circumstances, it dawned on me that the Mutt and Jeff saga had ultimately been about the power of *attitude*.

The trial of facing Mutt and Jeff every day at the red pole was static, intense, and uncontrollable by me. My feelings and emotions had run the gamut. I had gone from fear to anger, then indifference, and finally humor—yet their actions had never changed. In a random and unconscious way, my attitude about them had steadily changed, and, ultimately, it was the power of my attitude that surmounted the problem and made it go away.

The realization came to me that I could consciously and purposely harness the power of a positive attitude and that I could use it as a dominant tool in meeting and overcoming challenges I would face on my unique flight to success.

In aviation, attitude is defined as the orientation of an aircraft's axis, up or down. It determines whether you are climbing and flying that airplane to greater heights or—if you don't eventually make an adjustment—whether you're headed down straight for the ground. Attitude also determines whether you are turning left or right, which ultimately determines if you will be headed in the correct direction for where you want to go.

In life, attitude has a much broader meaning. Generally, it defines our outlook on a certain thing in particular or on how we view the world. Our attitude can touch our life in very different and unforeseen ways. My Mutt and Jeff experience showed in a very real sense how attitude can affect and even alter our external environment and our circumstances. Our attitude also defines how we feel about ourselves. The attitudes we have about ourselves can have an even more powerful effect—either good or bad—on where we end up.

*"If your attitude about yourself is
self-limiting, then you'll be self-limited!"*

Most of us have had self-doubts about who we are, where we are, what we are doing, or where we are going at some juncture in life. When we experience these moments of doubt, we often find ourselves coupling those uncertain feelings with self-limiting language. How many times have you said or thought, "I could never do that . . . can't even see myself . . . couldn't even imagine doing . . ."? I'll let you fill in the blanks. What we fail to realize is that most of our self-doubts are only false limitations we put on ourselves. They are not true limitations. If your attitude about yourself is self-limiting, then you'll be self-limited! It is a self-fulfilling prophecy!

My roommate at the Air Force Academy during the first semester of freshman year was a fellow football player from Southern California. Exuding that West Coast style, he was a pretty laid-back guy, and as starters on the freshman team, we got along reasonably well. Late in the fall after the football season was over, he transitioned to his favorite winter sport, skiing, which took him to the Colorado mountains on our limited free weekends. His sojourns included Aspen, Vail, and Winter Park in Colorado, and he often returned with stories about how fantastic the snow had been and what a great time he had had.

As a young black kid from South Carolina, I had grown up seeing very little of the white stuff and with a totally different attitude about snow. In my world, an inch of snow was a state of emergency and a day out of school, and so his animated exclamations about his skiing weekends were of little interest to me. You'll understand, then, why I was quick to turn down his invitation when he asked me to go skiing with him.

Not only were my experiences with and feelings about snow totally different from his, but also my attitude about participating in a sport that required being out in the snow the entire time was wholly unenthusiastic. Black kids played football and basketball. I couldn't even imagine skiing. Besides, I didn't like being out in the cold, so I knew without a doubt that skiing was not for me. My attitude caused a self-limiting mindset concerning something I knew absolutely nothing about.

To his credit and my ultimate benefit, my roommate didn't give up on me, and over time he countered all of my objections on why I wouldn't go skiing with him.

"I can't ski," I told him.

"I used to be a ski instructor. I'll teach you," he said.

"I don't like being miserable out in the cold," I said.

"The humidity is different than it is in South Carolina, and you won't feel the cold," he shot back. "Besides, we'll dress you the right way, and you'll probably be so warm you'll want to take stuff off."

"I don't have any equipment," I stated.

"You can get everything you need from the Cadet Ski Club for five dollars," he said, "and a discounted ski ticket. I know you'll enjoy it, and you'll be good at it, and if I'm wrong, you'll never have to go again."

I reluctantly, skeptically, and unenthusiastically went skiing with him one weekend soon thereafter and had the time of my life! The experience was challenging but exhilarating, and the scenery was absolutely breathtaking. I've been an avid skier ever since.

Your attitude about yourself drives most of the decisions you make in life. As you make choices that will determine your flight path, it is crucial to understand that we are all biased in some ways and see the world through filters, like my filtered boyhood view of snow. There are many causes for our biases: our personalities, our families and cultural environments, our lifestyles, and experiences—all of which combine to form our beliefs. It's crucial that we recognize these biases and take them into account when we make fundamental decisions about the things that are important in our lives.

If you think about it, your attitude affects every aspect of your being and has profound effects on your entire life. It determines your mental, emotional, physical, and financial states. If you have an attitude that you could never be wealthy, then you never will be. If you make excuses for why you are not healthy and why you can't be slim and in shape, then you'll continue to be dissatisfied with your appearance. If your attitude about your job allows it to dominate your life, then it's possible you won't have time for yourself or your family or the opportunity to enjoy the simpler—and often finer—things in life.

Your attitude controls what you think about and how you act and react. It is amazingly significant in determining how you project: It is the mirror of your mind, and people can often look at you and tell by your expressions and body language how you feel.

Attitude influences your posture and body movements and impacts how you look and feel. When you are dejected, your shoulders slump and your head hangs down, and you tend to walk a little slower. But when you walk tall and proudly with a confident look and a big smile on your face, it's tough to feel down. At the Air Force Academy we were told to "stand tall; stomach in; chest out; shoulders back and down." In addition to making us look good, a sharp appearance instilled personal pride, which helped to keep our confidence high. Fighter pilots are often called "cocky" and are known to have a certain confident "attitude." They believe they are the best pilots in the world, and history and performance have proven that US fighter pilots are just that.

———

It is easy to say, "Have a positive attitude." Pulling that attitude off may be a bit challenging, particularly when life may not be giving you its best. But there are things you can do to help build that ability over time. Here are some insights to help you along on your remarkable flight.

IT'S ALL A MIND GAME

The first and most important notion to both understand and master is that attitude is all mental. It is literally a mind game. You win by accepting and acting on the reality that ultimately you have the power to control how you feel. Of course, very often in life you can't control events, circumstances, or other things that may happen to you. But you can always choose how you react to them.

ACTING POSITIVELY

Concentrate on being positive. The more you think about and focus on being positive, the better you will become at generating and controlling positive thoughts. Like most skills, the more you do it and the harder you practice, the better you will become. In time, it will become your natural habit. Habits are learned and become our normal behaviors by extensive repetition.

SPEAKING POSITIVELY

Speak in a positive way. You control how you communicate. If you can—without lying, of course, or being unauthentic—put a positive spin on things whenever possible. Get rid of the self-limiting talk. If you say you can't do something, then guess what? You won't be able to! Speak well of others and don't be quick to criticize. Treat folks as you would like to be treated and remember what your mom taught you: If you can't say something nice about someone, then don't say anything at all.

NO ONE LIKES A WHINER

Don't be a whiner. Nobody likes one, wants to be around one, or wants to help one out. Most people don't like to be with someone who is complaining all the time and doesn't have anything positive to give to the conversation or the situation. If someone asks, "How is your day going?" focus on the good and minimize the bad. No one wants to hear bad stuff or all about others' problems. They want to hear the good stuff.

TURN THAT FROWN . . .

Be enthusiastic and try to keep a smile on your face whenever you have the right opportunity. You have to be enthusiastic if you want to generate enthusiasm in others. Science actually proves that it is easier to smile than to frown. Think about the things in life that make you happy. A smile will come naturally when you think about all the positive things you have to be thankful for.

COMPLIMENT FREELY

Be generous with compliments. When you offer praise to someone, it generates an immediate, positive, and often cheerful response. We all want to be acknowledged and appreciated for who we are or the things we do. When you give those kind words of value, you can inspire, motivate, and immediately brighten up someone's day. Abraham Lincoln, arguably our greatest president, believed in spreading positive energy and was big on complimenting people. He once confided to his friend Thurlow Weed,

"Everybody likes a compliment."[2] But here is the secret: Giving the compliment often makes you feel even better because the recipient's happiness reflects back on you. The old saying, "What goes around comes around," is clearly applicable here.

OWN UP

Admit it when you are wrong, and concede when you don't know something—even if it's hard to do. Some folks believe that admitting you're wrong indicates weakness or ineptness. In reality, refusing to acknowledge a mistake can be what shows weakness of character or low self-confidence. Conversely, admitting a mistake or acknowledging that you are not all-knowing provides an opportunity to learn while you end up building your credibility in the process. Besides, if you stick to your erroneous guns, you are likely to be criticized, and it's always better to criticize yourself than to have others criticize you.

THE SUNNY SIDE

Look at the brighter side of life. No matter how bad a situation may seem at the time, there is usually some good that can come out of it. I was in a serious accident and totaled my car last year, but luckily no one was injured (good #1), and I subsequently bought a new Tesla Model S and discovered what driving in the future will be like, today (good #2). What a phenomenal experience! If not for the bad event, I would never be experiencing the sublime drive today.

2　Donald T. Phillips, *Lincoln on Leadership: Executive Strategies for Tough Times* (New York: Warner Books, 1993), 18.

BE CHOOSY

Choose to be around positive people. They tend to enjoy life more, exude confidence, and experience greater levels of success. These are the types of folks you want as your fellow pilots or in your flight crew. The old proverb "Birds of a feather flock together" is still good and wise advice.

Not only can a positive attitude lead to more happiness and greater overall success in life, but there may actually be instances where the right outlook can lead to direct financial reward too. The right attitude can help you get that dream job or a favored promotion, or contribute to longer-term job security.

CHECK IT AT THE DOOR

I have a good friend who has enjoyed a successful legal and corporate career at the highest levels of business and government. He has been a kind and enthusiastic mentor of mine over the years and has also helped open doors for me.

Some years ago, he called to tell me that he had recommended me to be on the board of directors of a financial institution based in Boston. The CEO of the company was a friend of his and had reached out to him for some suitable recommendations. My friend told me that he had given the CEO a few names but had listed me as his number one choice. He told me to expect a call from the CEO sometime in the not-too-distant future.

As expected, I received the call about a week later, and the CEO and I had a very pleasant and somewhat lengthy conversation. At the end of the call, he invited me to lunch so we could meet in person and he could introduce me to a couple of other key board members. The lunch was enjoyable and the conversation was easygoing, with the CEO saying that he would be contacting me in the near future to follow up.

Several days later, the CEO called to say that he and the other board members had really enjoyed meeting me at our lunch and had been very impressed with both the conversation and my career. Notwithstanding his compliments, he also told me they had decided to go with another person for the seat on the board.

To say that I was stunned and shocked would be an understatement, and what immediately followed was a huge wave of disappointment. Knowing that my friend had recommended me as his number one choice and that I had had a great interview and lunch had given me the false assumption that I would be chosen for the position. I hadn't even considered any alternative. As I dejectedly began to thank the CEO for his consideration, he interrupted and said that they still wanted me to be a part of the company by serving on an advisory board.

I thought I had left it at the door but found that it was right there with me on the phone call—my ego. As the singer Alanis Morissette once said, "The ego is a fascinating monster." Having been rejected for a position that I fully expected to have, I was feeling hurt, and I felt snubbed to be offered what was clearly a significantly lesser position. I politely but decisively told the CEO that I was better suited for a decision-making role and didn't think the advisory board position would be a fit for me. He reiterated his desire to have me involved with the company and suggested that I think more about it and let him know in a couple of days. I halfheartedly agreed to his suggestion, knowing in my heart that my decision would not change.

I called my mentor to bring him up to date on the goings-on and to thank him for having recommended me. I also told him about the advisory board offer and my intention to turn it down. He wisely suggested that I give that decision more thought, and we talked about it a bit more. At the end of our discussion, it was clear to me that my ego had gotten the best of me, and there were some very good reasons to accept the advisory board offer. With the monster back in check, I called the CEO and told him that I would be honored to accept the advisory board position and that I was very appreciative for his gracious offer.

Having accepted the CEO's offer, I decided to change my attitude of disappointment and be the best advisory board member I could be. I attended all the meetings and other corporate functions. I followed the company in the financial news and sent short notes of congrats to the CEO and other senior officers when we had significant accomplishments or met or exceeded goals. I was asked to serve on a committee and enthusiastically agreed to do so, and I did my best to make a positive contribution. I was happy that I had made the decision to come on board.

About a year into my advisory board tenure, I was invited to lunch with the CEO and the senior vice president for business development. I knew there was an expectation that the board of directors and advisory board members would do business with the company, and I had made a conscious effort to do so. Yet I had also done similar business with another company that I had a long-standing relationship with and felt obligated to continue to do some of my business with them. I expected to be asked to increase the amount of business that I was doing with my new company.

After an enjoyable lunch and good conversation, I waited for the increased business pitch to come. The CEO began by commenting on what a good advisory board member I had been. He also thanked me for the periodic messages I had sent and noted my keen knowledge of what was being reported in the press on the company. He specifically mentioned the positive attitude I had shown in joining the company after not being invited to serve on the board of directors. Still waiting for the pitch, I was shocked when he surprisingly said, "We have a member who is retiring unexpectedly, and we would like you to become our newest member of the board of directors."

Needless to say, I accepted the invitation. The board appointment was an educational and enjoyable experience that enabled me to meet some wonderful people over my long tenure. I did business that was not related to the company with other members, and the board compensation was quite generous. I can directly attribute the personal and financial success I enjoyed with the company to having put the ego monster back in its cage and making a conscious decision to change my attitude.

We all have to fly through turbulent skies at different times in our lives. Things won't always go our way, and we'll be terribly disappointed with the outcome or the situation we find ourselves in. The key to succeeding during these times is not avoiding dealing with adversity, but rather, how fast you can bounce back from it. In the aviation business, we call this the rate of recovery. If your aircraft stalls, you have to recover and recover fast to get it flying again. If you don't, you'll run the risk of getting in a downward spiral where you are guaranteed to crash and burn.

Having a positive attitude in dealing with life's challenges is akin to executing a quick, smooth, and precise stall recovery. You'll immediately get your plane flying again with a minimum loss of altitude. Once you are stable, you can then push up the power and begin to climb.

Your attitude controls your altitude and determines how high you can soar. The captain has to keep the inevitable challenges, which most certainly will arise, in their proper perspective. In most cases, things can always be worse. Having a positive attitude enables optimistic, creative, and productive thinking when you are dealing with the everyday trials of life. A positive attitude is also contagious and will positively affect other members of your flight crew. Your positive attitude will be indispensable in attaining excellence and achieving your goals.

=PART II=

PEOPLE

"Only by attracting the best people will you accomplish great deeds."

—COLIN POWELL,
American statesman
and retired four-star general

PICK YOUR FLIGHT
CREW WISELY

WHEN I WAS a young boy, I was free to roam the neighborhood—just like all the other kids on my block. We played as a group almost every day, and our families knew one another intimately. We went from home to home as if each was our own. It was a close-knit community where our parents socialized, and the kids were together in school and after school got out.

One block up and two blocks over was another small community that had some kids who were about my age. I knew a couple of those kids, and I would sometimes "sneak" over to their neighborhood to play. To be honest, those kids were a little rougher than my neighborhood friends, and our playing sometimes pushed the envelope. That's to say that we did some things that I knew my parents wouldn't approve of; I can clearly remember the BB-gun battles we used to have. (Back in my neighborhood, parents would caution us about gun safety, responsibility, and never pointing a gun at another person.)

I was constantly surprised that my mom always seemed to know when I had been in that neighborhood, and I never knew exactly how she figured it out. It took me some time to realize all she had to do was just look at me to see where I had been. That neighborhood's streets were unpaved, and I would come home dusty and dirty from my rough play. She'd say, "You have been playing with those 'dirt road' boys again." I would always fess up, because I knew the penalty for telling a lie at my house. Her usual refrain was, "Show me your friends, and I'll show you your future." It was her shorthand way of telling me that I shouldn't be playing with kids who were likely to get me in more trouble than I was already prone to getting into on my own.

> *"Show me your friends, and*
> *I'll show you your future."*

As time passed, my mother's admonitions proved to be true. A couple of my "dirt road" buddies ended up dropping out of high school, and a couple more had what we called back then "run-ins with the law." Mom never said anything derogatory about those kids specifically, other than to say they were not the right kids to be playing with. Perhaps she had witnessed some interactions with the kids or their parents and didn't like what she saw. As a public elementary school teacher, she had forty-plus years of experience sorting out both parents and young kids.

In any event, my mother's intuition or knowledge was right on point. In my neighborhood, all of the kids finished high school, most went to college, and many ended up doing reasonably well.

The people you hang around with can have a marked effect on what you do with your life. The age-old debate of genes versus environment, more commonly called nature versus nurture, is still being discussed today. Yet most behavioral scientists acknowledge that despite our hereditary traits, we are in great part products of our environment. For example, the economic circumstances into which we are born can have a major effect on our longer-term opportunities for success. Access to financial resources may affect not just our dialect, but also our diet, education, and interests—and greatly influence how we perceive the world. Over time, early economic advantage can mark the paths we are likely to take. Will we finish high school or have run-ins with the law? Will we go to college and get a good job or work for minimum wage? Or possibly have no job at all? Will a stable environment determine whether we are more likely to get married, buy a house, have kids, and live the quintessential American Dream?

The fact is your associations can dramatically sway your values, and my mom was right to be concerned about the people I associated with and was influenced by. Today we are bombarded with countless questionable influences. Some are of the human persuasion, and others come to us through traditional and all sorts of evolving social media. Who we spend time with and what we see, read, hear, and otherwise learn have a tremendous effect on how we act and what we will become over time. Look at the people around you. Are they negative, complaining, do-nothing people? Or are they positive, confident, achievement-oriented folks? Do they share your principles, ideas, and values, or are they pulling you off track? There was a reason Mom kept saying, "Show me your friends, and I'll show you your future."

YOU'RE THE CAPTAIN

As you pilot your Flight to Excellence, it is critically important to realize that as the captain, you are in control of the ship. It is your job to pick your flight crew wisely. The people you choose to surround yourself with will go a long way in determining your business, your career, and ultimately your personal success. Let me emphasize that when I say *surround yourself*, I mean just that—people with authority over you, your colleagues and close friends, and the people you may one day end up leading. You'll want people who share your principles, ethics, and standards at every level. You want to encircle yourself with positive-thinking, intelligent, motivated people—ultimately, people who have your best interests at heart.

CHOOSING YOUR BOSS

In your professional life or career, you want to *choose* to work for a good boss, in a good company. When I've stated this notion in speeches or other conversations, people who don't believe you can actually choose your boss often challenge me. While I acknowledge that many folks *don't* choose a good boss, it's not correct to say you can't. In my entire professional career, I have only had one unsuitable boss, and I made the decision to work for him. And even in that situation, he wasn't a bad person. We just clashed on fundamental management style.

When I left the Air Force to pursue an airline career, I was living in Sacramento, California, and thoroughly enjoying the area with all it had to offer. I wanted to stay in the region, and I went looking for an airline company that would be a good fit for me.

As I did the research, I discovered I had several options at the time: American, United, Western, and Continental all had San Francisco pilot bases, and they became the objects of my focus. But as I dug deeper, I also discovered that there were some significant issues with all of those companies that I found unappealing—particularly with respect to financial viability and employee relations and retention. Reluctantly, I realized I needed to cast a wider net, even if it meant leaving the area I had grown to love.

In evaluating the remaining major airlines, Delta Air Lines, based in Atlanta, Georgia, stood out as the cream of the crop. The company had a stellar financial record. In addition, Delta had inculcated a culture of treating its employees like family and had never furloughed or laid off any of its pilots. Delta and its senior management team had been highlighted in both *Forbes* and *Business Week* magazines, and the "Delta Family" moniker was prominently featured in the articles.

But I had grown up in the South and didn't really have a desire to return to that part of the country for my career. Yet it was obvious to me that for my long-term job security and well-being, I'd have to give up my home base on the West Coast, hopefully only temporarily. And so I decided to try to get hired by Delta, which was a good company with an environment where people were valued. In short, I *chose* to have a good boss. The rest, as they say, is history, and I had wonderful chief pilots as bosses during my entire Delta career.

CHOOSING YOUR FRIENDS
AND CONTEMPORARIES

Just as you can choose your boss, you'll also want to carefully choose your friends and colleagues. You'll want to pick friends who are supportive in both practical and emotional settings, and who will be there for you when you need them. I have four best friends; I can literally count them on one hand. They live in different cities across the country, and here is what I know about their commitment to me: I could call any one—or all of them—and say I needed them in Atlanta right away. I could say, "I'll tell you why when you get here," and I am absolutely positive that all four would catch the next flight out.

We all have our good days and bad days, our ups and downs. True friends will be there to support you, celebrate your victories, and help you get through the difficult times. They will be there to applaud an entrepreneurial start-up or stand by you through career disappointments and business setbacks. They will be with you during the highs of the engagements and the lows of the breakups and divorces. Your best friends will become the god-parents for your kids and stand by you when you have to say good-bye to close family members for the last time.

You want friends you can communicate with on the most basic level, with no pretensions or inhibitions. You have to be totally comfortable with each other and be willing to discuss any topic—even when you might spiritedly disagree. You need friends who will tell you the truth and who will be brutally honest with you, even when it's something you don't want to hear. And when you have those rare dustups, true friends apologize to each other, let it go, and move on.

My bar for true friendship is exceedingly high, but I also

have many other folks I am very friendly with. You'll usually find colleagues or contemporaries in your work or professional environment or perhaps in social or nonprofit activities that you may be involved in. I have strong and wonderful relationships with many of my close associates, but my expectations of and obligations toward them are different from those I have with my friends. Just as with choosing a boss or best friends, you should only associate with quality people who are worth the time and effort it takes to develop a meaningful relationship with.

It is also critically important that you share the same principles—or conflict is likely to occur. When I founded the Summit Group, a financial consulting business, most of my initial clients were doctors and fellow airline pilots with whom I had personal relationships. Our company's goal was to provide them with the best tax and financial advice available and to save them as much money as possible. I soon discovered that insurance was an area we also needed to address, but insurance was a competency I didn't possess. I turned to a gentleman I served with on a nonprofit board. He was a personable guy and very competent in the insurance field. We had spent time together socially with our spouses, and I believed he might be the perfect fit for my business.

We agreed to work together in a collaborative relationship, and in the beginning, things worked out fine. As time progressed, however, I realized that the insurance products we were providing our clients were higher-cost options. While we made more money on them, we could have offered equally suitable products at a much lower cost. Our company goal was to save our clients as much money as possible, and these higher-cost products were incompatible with that goal. His goal was to maximize income on the insurance products, so our principles were not in alignment. Needless to say, the business relationship did not survive over time.

CHOOSING THE PEOPLE YOU LEAD

When I first interviewed with Delta Air Lines for my job as a pilot, I distinctly remember the conversation with Dr. Sidney Janus, the psychologist employed by Delta to interview potential new pilots. Dr. Janus was famous in the "want-to-be" airline pilot community, and everyone knew that to be hired by Delta, you had to make it through his interview. He had a rocking chair in his office, and part of the lore had to do with whether you rocked or sat still in the chair, which was supposed to have some psychological insight into your fitness for employment with Delta. I did sit in the rocking chair because it was the seat he offered, but I don't remember whether I rocked or not. It turns out that the chair was given to him by his wife, which was the only reason it was there.

We talked at length about the type of person Delta wanted to fly their airplanes and the characteristics of the people who would ultimately be offered employment as an entry-level second officer. Focusing on the integrity and leadership qualities required by Delta, Dr. Janus summed up our conversation by saying, "We only hire captains at Delta, people who will be excellent at leading their flight crews. It's just going to take you some years before you actually get to the captain's seat. I'll look forward to following your career."

Needless to say, I was very pleased to make it through the interview with Dr. Janus, but the larger point here is that Delta was deliberate and meticulous about hiring the types of people they wanted as its pilots. You'll need to be as particular with your flight crew. You'll want your team members in the business unit, or your working group, to have the types of values and character-istics you deem important and be able to work as a team. If you are an entrepreneur, you'll probably begin your venture having to hire your own employees, and you'll want a process to ensure you get people with the qualities you want and need. Your focus on this must be intentional because it is too important to be left to chance. Leading individuals is often your greatest challenge, and it significantly helps to have the right kind of people to lead.

CHOOSING A MASTERMIND GROUP

I have a substantial personal library, and a major part of my col-lection is made up of books on leadership, self-help, and financial success. While I have enjoyed reading most of them, my all-time favorite in those categories is a book written in 1937 by Napoleon Hill entitled *Think and Grow Rich*. I don't necessarily believe in or practice every one of the concepts outlined in the book, but it provides an excellent foundation and "flight plan" for achieving success in your business or personal life.

I've applied many of its concepts, and I find that rereading it periodically gives me a recharge as I take on any new adventure in life. I reread it every three or four years and have given copies to my daughters and others who are close to me. I firmly believe it has been one of the more important catalysts for my own personal success.

One of the important and powerful concepts in *Think and Grow Rich* is that of a "Master Mind." Hill defined the master-mind principle as the "coordination of knowledge and effort, in a spirit of harmony, between two or more people, for the attainment of a definite purpose." Hill learned about success and cooperation in mastermind groups by studying successful Americans such as Thomas Edison, Henry Ford, Andrew Carnegie, John D. Rockefeller, and Alexander Graham Bell. He saw how they worked together with their close networks and gained tremendous wealth and power.

When it comes to surrounding yourself with the right people—and wisely choosing your flight crew—forming or becoming a part of an existing mastermind group can be a tremendously powerful tool. A modern-day mastermind group is a peer-to-peer mentoring concept in which members share knowledge and focus on their goals, seek and provide advice to each other, help solve problems, and ultimately accomplish their objectives. If you seek out a group of smart people who work together, everyone will be able to move collectively forward. Such a group normally meets on a regular basis, usually weekly or monthly, and you can use those sessions to develop and strengthen relationships and to tackle the challenges facing you.

If you would like to join an existing mastermind group, there are a host of opportunities, with the fastest and most direct avenue for information being the online option. Search the specific area you are interested in, and you are sure to find a plethora of possibilities. There are masterminds for business start-ups, small businesses, businesswomen, entrepreneurs, innovation, and the list goes on. You will also find masterminds for specific positions, like CEOs and CFOs, and masterminds for specific disciplines like marketing or finance.

Businesses such as Vistage host mastermind groups, and other organizations have mastermind components. The YPO (Young Presidents' Organization) and the EO (Entrepreneurs' Organization) are two widely known and reputable groups. Finally, there are specific services that provide a listing of mastermind groups.

The Success Alliance website is an excellent source for valuable information on how to start your own mastermind group if you are so inclined.

There are many advantages of being in a well-functioning mastermind group. The first and most obvious advantage is that by being part of a group, you're not dealing with issues alone and unaided. Being an entrepreneur, for example, can be a lonely game, and it helps to know that you can share and discuss options with others who are people of substance with exceptional knowledge or backgrounds. Most mastermind groups have a screening process to ensure that the members are all bringing value to the table.

Being in a mastermind group is not right for everyone, and every mastermind group doesn't work out. But being a member of an effective group can give you the opportunity to grow your personal and online network. You may be able to share lists or be introduced to a key person who can substantially move you forward. There may also be opportunities to do business with other members of the group. Finally, because different skill sets of members may mesh perfectly in a collaborative and profitable way, joint ventures or partnerships may be an unexpected positive result.

CHOOSING TO MOVE ON

On one occasion when I was in my hometown visiting my mom and dad, I ran across a classmate from high school. It was great to see him after so many years, and I enjoyed the time we spent catching up on our lives. As we wrapped up our unexpected visit, he asked if I ever thought I'd move back home. Before I could answer his question, he provided an answer for me. "Given your experiences and the different things you've done, I could never see you living back here again. You have outgrown Orangeburg."

The truth is I love my hometown and have maintained strong connections there. I visit my relatives often and serve on the board of trustees of the local university. Yet my friend raised a valid issue, which many people have found to be the case: As you grow and advance in both your personal and professional life, you'll leave certain people and places behind. In some cases this will be a conscious choice, as you come to realize that your principles and standards are not the same. In other cases it becomes inevitable, as your interests, goals, and opportunities change. As long as there is no malicious intent, accept that this is part of the natural order of growth, development, and maturity in life.

POETRY IN MOTION

This chapter has been about the importance of picking the right people to surround yourself with in your life and career. If we've done our job correctly, we have a well-functioning, high-performing team that is a wonderful thing to behold. Watching the perfect team in action is like experiencing "poetry in motion," as the old phrase goes. It's like seeing someone or something that moves in a way that is full of grace and beauty.

As the captain of your ship, you have the opportunity, the power, and the responsibility to write your own poetry by thoughtfully choosing the people who surround you—by selecting a topflight crew.

LET YOUR COPILOTS FLY

"Everybody needs a co-pilot."

—GEORGE CLOONEY,
playing the part of Ryan Bingham
in *Up in the Air*

IN THE AIRLINE business, the captain, by federal law, is in complete charge of the airplane. She has the overall responsibility for the safe and efficient operation of the flight and the safety of the crew and passengers. Sitting right next to the captain is the trusted copilot. His job is to assist the captain in conducting the flight and to take over if for some reason the captain becomes incapacitated.

While the leadership responsibilities clearly rest with the captain, the actual cockpit duties for both the captain and the copilot are quite similar. In fact, at most major air carriers, the captain and the copilot actually switch most duties every other leg of the flight. For example, when one pilot is flying the jet, the other pilot handles navigation and communication duties. On the next flight, the responsibilities reverse. Practically speaking, while the captain is the captain, the captain and the copilot collectively perform all of the flight duties and functions as a well-coordinated team.

As a young copilot at Delta, I would, on rare occasions, fly with a captain who had a reputation for not letting the copilot fly his share of the time, and those were not enjoyable three- or four-day trips. On each day we might fly into two to four different cities across the country. Only handling the radios and talking with the air traffic controllers while managing the navigation without having the opportunity to fly the airplane was quite boring and made for a long day at work. Because not sharing the flight duties was against Delta's policy, I made it a point to stop by the chief pilot's office for a conversation when I infrequently ran into this situation. My reason for doing this was that I hoped the next copilot to fly with that captain would have a better and safer overall experience if the chief pilot got involved.

The policy of the captain and the copilot alternating duties every other leg was instituted so the copilot could share some of the workload. But more important, it is so the copilot can gain flying proficiency and decision-making experience on the way to becoming a captain. Reversing roles gives the captain the opportunity to observe and coach the copilot while helping him refine his performance, techniques, and decision-making abilities. Obviously, if the copilot isn't allowed to fly, both his aviation skills and executive development are severely impacted.

This leadership and expertise-development process is one of the reasons the modern airline business sustains such a phenomenal safety record and functions consistently with a high degree of operational excellence. When both pilots maintain an exceptional level of flying ability and work closely together, they accomplish a challenging, highly technical, and crucially important goal. A copilot who is under the tutelage of an accomplished captain is learning to make decisions. Making the right decisions increases his judgment capabilities and ultimately contributes to the safe and efficient operation of any flight.

IMPLEMENTING EMPOWERMENT

Unfortunately, in many other areas of business today, leaders are not giving their people the opportunity to make meaningful decisions or to sharpen their skills in a way that positively affects the outcome of the ventures. To be fair, the traditional top-down approach where employees are told by management what to do and how to do it has worked for eons. Yet, in more recent times, enlightened leaders have discovered the benefits of involving their employees in both the decision-making and implementation aspects of the business.

To become and to remain competitive in today's fast-paced business environment, it is critically important to trust your people to make routine decisions within reasonable boundaries. Excellent leaders empower their people by giving them opportunities to be innovative and creative, and to contribute to the organization in meaningful ways. Not only does this motivate talented employees by expanding their horizons, but it also encourages them to do more, to achieve more, and to be more—which ultimately benefits the organization.

For example, at the Summit Group, the company I founded,

we empowered our unit managers to run their own marketing campaigns rather than impose a top-down corporate operation. One of our Subway stores won the Subway systemwide award for the most innovative marketing program, in a collaborative campaign with the hockey team at Northeastern University in Boston. The prize was an all-expenses-paid trip for two to the Sarajevo Winter Olympics. We sent that store's top two managers to enjoy the European adventure.

Both psychological and business studies have documented the positive effect that empowering employees has on both the enterprise and the employee/crew member. The authors of a 2011 study noted that empowered employees had greater job satisfaction, increased commitment to the organization, and performed at a higher level, while at the same time, personal stress and turnover in the organization were reduced.[3] Moreover, the study found that team empowerment related directly to team performance.

In a 2018 *Harvard Business Review* article,[4] researchers wrote that leaders who empower their employees find they behave in a much more creative fashion and are more likely to engage in "citizenship behavior." The authors defined citizenship behavior as behavior that is not formally recognized or rewarded—such as helping coworkers or attending work functions that aren't mandatory. The study also found that leaders who empower their employees are more likely to be trusted by their people, compared to leaders who do not empower their employees.

---

3   Scott Seibert, Gang Wang, and Stephen Courtright, "Empowerment Is Everything! What Does It Take?" *Journal of Applied Psychology*, September/October 2011.

4   Allan Lee, Sara Willis, and Amy Wei Tian, "When Empowering Employees Works, and When It Doesn't," *Harvard Business Review*, March 2, 2018.

Trust is critical to any empowering effort, because it enables a leader to create a secure and safe environment where employees feel assertive enough to make the most of the empowerment opportunity. When conditions feel safe, employees are self-confident and are more likely to engage and collaborate enthusiastically with both their colleagues and supervisors.

Of course, announcing that your crew members are now "empowered" is not nearly enough. It is also crucially important to ensure that your organization's policies, procedures, and guidelines are clear on what your employees are empowered to do. These documents should be written, in place, and readily available so that everyone is on the same page with respect to the rules of the game. Empowering your crew members may also require a greater knowledge of the business on their part and may generate a need for new or enhanced training to develop or improve their current skills.

WHAT REAL EMPOWERMENT LOOKS LIKE

In one of my entrepreneurial ventures, I was a multi-brand and multi-unit fast-food franchisee. The company, Summit Food Services, a division of the Summit Group, owned Dunkin' Donuts, TCBY, and Subway franchises in New England. Because I was running other businesses and flying for Delta, I didn't get to the stores on a regular basis as much as I would have liked to. As a result, we empowered our store managers to make many everyday decisions, like the marketing programs I mentioned previously.

While I didn't know all of my frontline food services crew members, I would put on a uniform and periodically go to the stores to work a routine shift. My friends would jokingly accuse me of being an "undercover boss," and there were certainly surprises to be had at times. But I always introduced myself using my real name, and other than wearing a uniform, I never wore any type of disguise.

I had returned from a Delta trip early on a Friday afternoon and decided to stop by the office to check on things rather than going straight home. My executive assistant, Lori Stoico, gave me a rundown on our business operations, and other than an employee calling in sick at one of the Subways, things were in pretty good shape. I decided I would go to that Subway (coincidentally, my very first store) and help the employee, a young lady named Paula, who was working the shift all alone. I put on my Subway shirt, grabbed my hat and apron, and headed on over.

When I arrived and walked into the store, the place looked great! The customer eating area was neat and clean, with the floor swept and the tables all wiped down. The bins were filled with freshly chopped vegetables, and Paula had just finished baking bread and chocolate chip cookies. An enticing aroma permeated the place.

I introduced myself and told her I was there to fill in for the crew member who had called in sick. It was clear to me that she didn't know who I was, and from my perspective, that was just fine. In fact, she thought I was a new employee, and she began to give me tips on how best to perform some of the store duties. I was very impressed with her willingness to take me under her wing and show me the ropes.

A while later, a gentleman walked in drinking a twenty-ounce bottle of Coke. He was one of my long-standing customers; I had seen him in the store numerous times over the years. He walked up to Paula and ordered a #3 from the menu—a foot-long sub, a bag of chips, and a drink of choice. Spying the freshly baked chocolate chip cookies on the counter, he said, "I don't need a drink, so I'd like one of those cookies instead."

Not missing the opportunity to upsell as she had been trained to do, Paula enthusiastically responded, "You'll like those cookies, and they are freshly baked, but I'll have to add it to your order because I can't make a substitution."

The customer studied the menu board for a moment and then asked, "Why not? A drink is listed at $1.09, and a cookie is only fifty-nine cents. I'm saving you fifty cents on that deal!"

As I observed and listened to their conversation, I also wondered why Paula wouldn't make what seemed to be a reasonable request. The guy had his Coke and obviously didn't need another soda, and the cookie was a lower-cost item to us compared to the drink. It seemed to be an easy request to grant.

Paula politely and professionally began to explain why she couldn't allow his request. She said, "Sir, the cash register is actually a computer that tracks all of our sales. The #3 is already programmed in. If I give you a cookie instead of a drink, and ring it up as a #3, I'll be a cookie short and a drink cup over when I do my end-of-shift report."

I immediately understood Paula's problem. While we had "empowered" our managers to make frontline decisions, we had also stressed the importance of our crew members properly and accurately completing our required paperwork. Our forms were the heart of the control system that enabled us to both track sales and prevent inventory waste and theft. In the present case, my policies and procedures were preventing Paula from making a commonsense decision to better serve one of our long-standing customers.

I stepped in at this point and told the gentleman that we

would be happy to give him a cookie instead of another Coke, and Paula immediately gave me a disapproving look. I asked her to trust that things would be all right as we finished serving what was now a satisfied customer. Shortly afterward, when we got a break from serving customers, I pulled Paula aside and told her who I was. To say that she was surprised would be an understatement. I complimented her on doing a great job running the store, and then I apologized to her.

Paula was a great crew member who was doing everything we had asked her to do, but as a leader, I had let her down. While I assumed that I had "empowered" my store managers, I discovered that because of my policies and procedures, our frontline crew members didn't have the power to make reasonable, common-sense decisions to better serve our customers. It was immediately apparent that I needed to make a change.

The following week we had a systemwide meeting of all store managers to discuss what I had observed and to identify other areas where our policies and procedures hindered better service to our customers. We were able to make several changes, which truly empowered our frontline folks with little impact on our need to track sales and address waste and fraud. Coincidentally, Paula's store went on to win the national award for the highest percentage of sales increase in the entire Subway system.

Photo © 2020 by Scott P. Youngblood

WHEN THE CAPTAIN IS UNQUESTIONABLE

The airline business in general, and the pilot side of the business in particular, is generally governed by strict seniority. The airplane you fly, the routes you fly, and the position you fly—whether captain or copilot—are all determined by your date of hire or seniority date. Delta's new pilots were all employed as flight engineers or second officers during the time when I was hired. This began a many-year ascension to copilot or first officer, followed by several more years before having the seniority to become a captain. Today's modern airliners have only two pilots, so the entry-level job is that of copilot, also called the first officer.

During my initial interview for a pilot's job with Delta, I

distinctly remember being told that Delta only hired captains. Being familiar with the seniority system, I guess I had a confused look on my face when I heard this. The interviewer laughed and repeated the statement. He then added, "It's just going to take you a while to get there."

When I got hired by Delta, it was known as a "captain's airline," which meant that the captains were highly respected and perceived to have great power and influence within the company. Delta was very selective about who they hired to be its future captains. I had many Air Force pilot friends who got interviews with other major airlines but didn't get interviews with Delta. Still others got interviews with Delta, but they didn't ultimately get hired. Fortunately, most of them were hired by other airlines and had successful careers. I also hasten to add that they were all very fine people and excellent pilots, and we often commiserated that there seemed to be little rhyme or reason about who Delta hired or didn't hire.

Over time, the captain's absolute authority began to become problematic at several major airlines and to a lesser extent at Delta as well. I say to a lesser extent at Delta, because the overwhelming majority of the captains I flew with in my copilot career were top-notch.

The authority problem for some captains centered on the tone they set in the cockpit. For the safe operation of a flight, it is important that the captain be open and use a collaborative leadership style. You want a captain who will ask for and receive feedback—regardless of what it is. If something in the cockpit doesn't look right, you want your copilot to speak up and be respectfully persistent until the issue is resolved. An authoritarian captain can set an atmosphere in the cockpit that ends up killing everyone on board.

This, unfortunately, has happened and has been documented as the cause of several major aircraft accidents—primarily with non-US carriers. The differences in cultural norms in some Asian and Latin American countries, where it is seen as disrespectful to question authority, have been a contributing factor in several major crashes. The KLM Flight 4805, Avianca Flight 52, and Korean Air Flight 801disasters all involved issues relating to a hesitancy to question authority. The Korean Air Flight 801 is particularly instructive, as the investigation showed that both the copilot and the flight engineer knew something was wrong at the time but were hesitant to aggressively challenge the captain. He decided to disregard their concerns and elected to continue the approach to landing. Because they were not vigorous in expressing their concerns, the captain crashed into the side of a hill, killing 228 of the 254 people on board.[5]

As a result of these crashes and other incidents, many airlines instituted a process called CRM or Crew Resource Management. The concept focuses on what had been the infallibility of the captain in the airline business. While retaining a command structure with complete captain authority, CRM focuses on a less authoritarian cockpit culture and encourages copilots to actively question captains if they observe them making mistakes. Top executives could use a similar program in business or in other organizations today.

---

5 Frank Swoboda, "Better Pilot Training Could Have Prevented Korean Air Crash, NTSB Says," *Washington Post*, November 3, 1999, https://www.washingtonpost.com/archive/politics/1999/11/03/better-pilot-training-could-have-prevented-korean-air-crash-ntsb-says/17821669-12f5-4ef4-a941-05ed220b3575/.

PARTNERS IN THE PROCESS: CRUCIAL COLLABORATION

An excellent leader, whether in business or in the cockpit, wants her crew members to be partners in the process and shouldn't want yes-men or yes-women who are hesitant to speak up when things don't look or feel right. Successful leaders will listen to their folks and create an environment where people can feel comfortable giving their honest input—and even challenging plans or actions in a respectful way. The captain wants her copilot to tell her when they are off course or about to land when the gear is not down and locked. CRM was designed to create this culture in the cockpit.

> *"An excellent leader . . . wants her crew members to be partners."*

On July 17, 1996, TWA Flight 800 blew up in the sky over the Atlantic Ocean shortly after taking off from John F. Kennedy International Airport in New York. All 230 souls on board perished in the accident. A week prior to the TWA tragedy, my Delta flight took off from John F. Kennedy International Airport in New York en route to Miami. Out over the Atlantic Ocean, abeam above the South Carolina coast, we received an emergency call from Delta Flight Control telling us that we had a credible threat of a bomb on board. Needless to say, the pucker factor went up to a very high level.

Fortunately, both the copilot and I had completed our CRM training, and we began to work on the problem as a coordinated team. I had been flying that leg of the trip, but I transferred control of the aircraft to the copilot so I could better manage the situation. I questioned flight control extensively to get as much factual data on the threat as I could. It was not the first time in my aviation career that my legal skills in interviewing had proven to be a big help. Given the information received, the copilot and I both agreed that the prudent course of action was to get the plane on the ground ASAP.

We decided to immediately divert to Charleston, South Carolina. Although we were a few miles closer to the Savannah airport, we picked Charleston because the distance was essentially the same, and more important, the Charleston airport shared its runways with Charleston Air Force Base, and we figured the Air Force would have better resources to handle a bomb situation.

After declaring an emergency with air traffic control, I called the flight attendant in charge up to the cockpit to brief her on our situation and to get her input on dealing with the passengers. We all agreed that it would be best to inform the passengers that we had a problem that required our diversion to Charleston but not to let them know the specific nature of the problem until after we landed. Assuming, of course, that we would actually be able to land.

With a plan in place and the key members of the team briefed, we executed our diversion to Charleston. We were particularly anxious as we descended through 18,000 feet—often called the transition altitude. All pilots receive bomb-threat training at Delta, and we learned that one of the techniques used by terrorists who would bomb an airliner is to include a triggering device to explode the bomb as it descends through a particular altitude. Given the importance of the transition altitude as a plane descends to land in the United States, it wasn't hard to imagine this as a possible point for an explosion. We made it through the transition altitude with a sigh of relief but clearly understood that until we got the airplane on the ground and everyone off and a safe distance away, we were still in jeopardy.

All other traffic was cleared out for our approach, and we landed with much fanfare in Charleston. The fire trucks, ambulances, and the Air Force bomb crew all met the flight as we quickly exited the runway and went to an isolated parking location. After a thorough search of the airplane, passengers, luggage, and cargo, it was determined that the threat was a hoax, and four hours later we were back on our way to South Florida.

The good news was that we worked the problem in a textbook way with all key crew members having input and smart suggestions to deal with a life-threatening problem. Of course, as the captain, I had the final say, but we had collaboratively discussed all the issues and reached consensus decisions that we were all comfortable with. The better news was that we hadn't been blown up in the middle of the sky!

My CRM training at the airline has proven to be a valuable addition to the leadership training I received at the Air Force Academy and during my active duty days in the Air Force. Yes, the leader is always the person in charge and bears the ultimate responsibility. But I have come to appreciate the immense value of input, creativity, and collaboration when members of the team are free to add to, adjust, and even challenge plans or assumptions that I may have about a particular course of action.

I have used the lessons learned in CRM training at Delta in both my business ventures at the Summit Group and during my tenure as president and CEO of the Association of Graduates (AOG) at the Air Force Academy. Creating a culture of collaboration that encourages imaginative input and empowering your crew members to challenge your assumptions, plans, or direction usually results in a much better product. Of course, being the leader means that the final decision and the responsibility rest with you. But your goal should always be to achieve the best possible result, and collaboration and empowerment are the secret ingredients to that end. Ultimately, proof of the effectiveness of this approach is clear in the consistent results achieved over time: numerous honors and millions of dollars made at the Summit Group, a plethora of awards and spectacular chapter and revenue growth at the AOG, and turnarounds and more efficient operation in the governmental sector.

Yes, the captain is always completely in charge. But truly, the sky is the limit when you let your copilots fly.

YOUR INSTRUCTOR PILOTS

> *"One of the greatest values of mentors*
> *is the ability to see ahead what others*
> *cannot see and to help them navigate a*
> *course to their destination."*
>
> **–JOHN C. MAXWELL,**
> American author, pastor, and leadership expert

I WAS EXCITED to be going to Valdosta, Georgia. But my close friends couldn't understand why.

I was about to begin what the Air Force calls Undergraduate Pilot Training (UPT) to earn my silver wings. I was glad to be heading back East to begin that yearlong training program at Moody Air Force Base. The Air Force also conducted the training at Williams Air Force Base near Phoenix, Arizona, and I had been given the opportunity to go through the program there. "Why would you want to be in the swamps of South Georgia when you could be in Phoenix?" my best friend asked.

Admittedly, it may seem strange, but I had my reasons.

Colorado is a beautiful state, but after four years at the Academy as a cadet, followed by an additional year on staff, I wanted something completely new. Colorado and Arizona have beautiful mountains, but I was ready to be within shorter driving distance of the ocean again. In addition, getting to see more of my mom and dad, who were in South Carolina within a moderate drive from the Georgia base, was a major motivation and an added treat.

And I actually had a strategic reason for my Georgia choice. I clearly understood that jet pilot training was going to be demanding, it would require my focused attention to complete, and I wanted and hoped to do well in the program. It would be best, I reasoned, not to have the distractions of the bustling nightlife in a city like Phoenix so close by. A periodic weekend trip home to get some of Mom's home cooking would do me just fine.

My pilot training class was known as "75-08"—the eighth class to start in 1975. Because I had spent time on staff at the Air Force Academy after graduation, I was the ranking second lieutenant (2nd Lt) in my class of newly minted second lieutenants or "butter bars," as the term is sometimes patronizingly used. It's military slang for the rank insignia for the 2nd Lt, which is a gold bar. Because of my rank, flight commander Captain Larry Strothers, who also became my instructor pilot (IP), appointed me section leader of the students in my class.

Captain Strothers was a Citadel graduate, and I shared with him that I was a South Carolinian who had almost become a cadet there before my Air Force Academy appointment came through. Of course, he was a captain, and I was a 2nd Lt: He was my instructor pilot, and I was his student pilot. As such, we never became good friends, nor did we socialize other than at official functions. Yet that small Carolina/Citadel bond seemed to break the ice, and it was clear to me from the beginning that he was committed to my becoming an Air Force pilot.

Captain Strothers's philosophy was that as the section leader, I should be out-front of the rest of the class. As a result, I flew more often than my classmates and moved through the syllabus at a faster pace. There were advantages and disadvantages to his approach. While it was good to be ahead of the program sched-ule, particularly when bad weather kept us grounded, there were major shortcomings to always doing things first.

The primary drawback was not having anyone else in your class who could tell you what was going on or what to expect in a particular phase of training. You had your instructor pilot to teach you, of course, but the student-to-student communication was invaluable as an unofficial "heads-up" asset. That responsibil-ity fell solely to me, and I saw how my experiences benefited my classmates, just as I understood how the lack of that same guid-ance played a role in my own training.

LAND THAT JET: WHY WE ALL NEED MENTORS

It was 1975, the year the Vietnam War officially ended. The country no longer needed pilots to fight a war, and hundreds of excess pilots were returning home. While there was never an offi-cial announcement of any sort to our class, several IPs confirmed that the program had become much more difficult to complete, as there was no longer a need for as many Air Force pilots as before.

The largest initial challenge in primary jet training is to land the aircraft safely. Taking off is relatively easy; getting back on the ground without killing yourself and your IP is where the rubber meets the runway. The other critical factor is time. I believe the majority of the student pilots who get to UPT could eventually learn how to land the jet safely. But the Air Force doesn't have an unlimited budget to teach you how to fly. If you can't "solo out" or fly by yourself within ten to twelve hours of flying time, you'll need to find another line of work—because you'll be out of UPT.

In order to solo out, your IP has to have the confidence that you can land safely. It is his call and his responsibility if you screw it up. (Well, I guess you have some responsibility too, but you may not be around to suffer the consequences.) If you break the jet or worse—you buy the farm—the ton of bricks will fall on your IP's head.

My first couple of rides in the program were great fun. Captain Strothers was doing a lot of demonstrating, and while I was also flying, expectations for me performing with a high degree of proficiency were low. That changed rapidly, though, and as I progressed through the syllabus, the expectations rose steeply. Additionally, as the section leader, I was expected to be the first in my class to solo, which meant that I had an added layer of pressure on me to be able to land that jet.

We were flying a traffic pattern–only flight to practice landings. Staying in the traffic pattern means taking off and immediately coming around to do a touch-and-go landing and then immediately taking off and repeating that, over and over again. My landings were a bit erratic, though occasionally I'd have what I considered to be a really good one. Then that might be followed by a landing where I bounced on the runway a couple of times, followed by one that I would slam down pretty hard. There were a couple of times when I decided I couldn't get the jet down on the runway. I had to "go around" to try it again. Overall, my skills were steadily improving, but I felt that I would need a lot more time—maybe three or four more rides—to get the landings just right and to solo out.

"If the boys back home could see me now!"

After an unexceptional landing, Captain Strothers told me to taxi the jet over to base operations, the building close to the runway that houses airfield operations. When we got there, he shut the right engine down, opened the cockpit canopy, and said, "You are ready to solo. Have fun." And then he got out of the airplane and walked into base ops. I was stunned and shocked! I wasn't ready to fly this jet by myself! And I was alone!

I had two choices: I could go park the jet or taxi back to the runway and fly it by myself. I chose the latter and had the time of my life. To this day, I can distinctly remember being in that cockpit alone, receiving my takeoff clearance and screaming out loud, "If the boys back home could see me now!" I was required to do three landings to complete my solo ride, and they were all pretty good. I taxied in, parked the jet, and then got out. I was met by waves of water from my classmates—an Air Force tradition of being doused upon completion of your first solo. It was a joyous day.

In talking with Captain Strothers, I asked him why he let me solo when I clearly thought I needed more rides. His comments were illuminating. Most important, he told me that I could safely fly the airplane. While all of my landings weren't perfect, they were safe, and that was the standard for a first solo. He also told me that I had shown good judgment when I had gone around for another try in situations when I decided I couldn't make a good landing. "It's no sin to try again," he said. "The sin is to try and land from an unsafe situation. You were ready, and you proved it today."

Captain Strothers was an excellent instructor pilot. He taught me well, guided me through the basic program, and had the confidence in me on several occasions when I thought I wasn't ready to tackle some aspect of the training. He pushed me to have high standards in the air and on the ground, and he added much to my professional development as both an officer and a pilot. We were not best of friends but were friendly, and he was focused on his job, which was to make me the best Air Force pilot I could be. In my opinion, he excelled in performing all of those duties.

Captain Larry Strothers was the first true mentor (in the professional sense) I had ever had. Of course, as is the case for most of us, my parents provided guidance. And we have close friends who give us advice—which is sometimes unsolicited and occasionally not very good. But even without a necessarily close personal relationship with him, I felt Captain Strothers was there for me. His job was to teach me how to fly a jet, and in doing that, he went above and beyond and took an interest in my success. The *Cambridge Dictionary* defines a mentor as "a person who gives a younger or less experienced person help and advice over a period of time, especially at work or at school." Captain Strothers fit this definition to a T and was a quintessential mentor who helped lay the foundation for my successful thirty-two-year professional aviation career.

Most of us can benefit tremendously from having strong, competent mentors in our lives. You shouldn't have to try to figure everything out by yourself. And as my relationship with Captain

Strothers demonstrated, a close personal relationship is not a prerequisite for a successful arrangement. The right mentor relationship can be the afterburner that accelerates your learning and helps propel your career progression or business achievements to fantastic heights. Captain Strothers was the perfect mentor for my aviation success, but key qualities of a great mentor that he embodied are universally applicable to career, business, or other endeavors.

KEY QUALITIES OF A GREAT MENTOR

➤ **A great mentor should have expertise and knowledge in your field of endeavor.**

It's important to have a mentor whose journey is complementary to yours and who has seen, done, or accomplished some of the things you are trying to achieve. They have probably been there and done that and can help keep you from making similar mistakes they had made. If you want to make partner in a large law firm, seek out a senior partner who understands the process and can help guide you along the track. If you want to become a successful fast-food franchisee, find a mentor who owns her own stores. She'll be in a better position to help you with the business and to advise you on how best to navigate the relationship with the corporate franchisor.

➤ **A great mentor will be invested in your success.**

While a close personal relationship is not required, your mentor has to have a strong interest in seeing you succeed.

continued

He will be invested in your achievements, much like a coach is invested in the success of his players. Often a mentor will take on a mentee as a way of giving back. She may have been mentored at a critical stage of her career and understands the value a mentor can provide.

> ➤ **A great mentor will provide honest and constructive feedback.**

A knowledgeable mentor will be able to help evaluate your strengths and weaknesses. He will help you see where you are deficient and where you need help to improve your skills. While always respectful and courteous, he will be brutally honest about what you need to do to progress.

> ➤ **A great mentor gives encouragement and emotional support.**

We all have our ups and downs and times when we are just drained because of the turbulence we have to navigate through. A good mentor will be there to offer support and reassurance and to help keep things in perspective when you are feeling overwhelmed. He can often see your potential when you don't see it in yourself.

> ➤ **A great mentor will act as an effective sounding board for your ideas.**

A great mentor will be a person you can trust to give you sound advice and honest opinions about the ideas you have and the route you may be taking or thinking of taking. When you are excited about a new concept or direction, it's extremely valuable to have someone who is not as emotionally engaged with your plan to give you that dispassionate critique.

> ➤ **A great mentor can be willing to share their network.**
>
> A great mentor may introduce you to folks who can help you out and shorten your learning curve. The people in their network may be able to do business with you, provide you with investment capital, or facilitate an employment opportunity at a higher level. Sharing a mentor's contact list may give you more marketing opportunities or introduce you to a completely new social set. You may end up in a world that you would otherwise never have been exposed to.

The right mentor can be an invaluable instructor pilot in your professional or business journeys. Several outstanding mentors in my life have been responsible for propelling my career, enhancing my business success, and even getting me involved in politics at the state and national level. Their invaluable advice and counsel and willingness to share resources, including key contacts, directly resulted in my financial and professional success.

YOU'VE LANDED THE JET: YOU STILL NEED AN INSTRUCTOR PILOT

Fast-forward from 1975 to 1980. Delta had just stationed me at my new pilot base in Boston. There may have been more attractive pilot base options for my Delta classmates, but I had ranked Boston as my first choice for one reason. I was in my last year of law school, and I figured that with six law schools in Boston at the time, I would be able to find one that would allow me to complete my final year of school.

On the last leg of a three-day trip back home to Boston, one of the Boston-based flight attendants, Karen, came into the cockpit. She was an experienced middle-aged African American woman who by appearance and demeanor exuded class and sophistication. Her reaction upon seeing me was mildly shocking and comical. "Where did you come from?" Karen asked. Apparently, I was one of only two African American pilots out of the four hundred Delta pilots stationed in Boston, and the other pilot lived in New York and commuted to Boston.

We chatted for a short while and she said, "I'm going to introduce you to the people you need to know in Boston. You are going to a party with me on Saturday afternoon." Being new to the city, I was all in.

That Saturday, we arrived at the home of a celebrated Harvard psychiatrist, Dr. Alvin Poussaint, who at the time was the consultant for *The Cosby Show*. Karen introduced me to the host and his wife and several other party guests. In a conversation with one of those guests who asked me how I had become an airline pilot, I mentioned that I had attended the Air Force Academy and flown in the Air Force before becoming a Delta pilot. He said, "There is another guy here who went to school at the Air Force Academy. Let me introduce you to him." And that is how I met Fletcher "Flash" Wiley, a 1965 graduate of the Academy and only the fifth African American to graduate from the school.

Flash was a prominent Boston lawyer who was very well established in the business community and connected politically. Fiercely loyal to the Academy, he immediately took me under his wing. He helped me with law school, and after I finished and passed the bar, I became "of counsel" to his firm on tax matters. Over time, he helped me in myriad other ways with real estate deals and my fast-food franchises. He introduced me to the governor, who subsequently appointed me as commissioner of aeronautics for the Commonwealth of Massachusetts.

As a lawyer and member of the bar, I was usually able to handle most legal matters associated with my entrepreneurial interests, but when things got serious or complicated, I turned to Flash. We developed a close friendship, and he eventually became the big brother I never had. He counseled me when I decided to get married and gave me advice when I was going through my divorce. He became the godfather of my firstborn child, and even today he is inextricably involved with my estate-planning affairs. Our relationship began as mentor/mentee but blossomed into so much more. It's the perfect example of the power of having a great mentor who possesses the key qualities I outlined earlier that I believe are crucial to attaining success.

A mentor can be a great educational resource as you focus on achieving your goals. In 1986, I had been recently elected to the state board of directors of the American Cancer Society. Stanley Shmishkiss, a major Boston businessman, was the chairman of the board. Stanley's idea was to get new board members involved quickly with board duties, and he asked me to serve on an important committee. I agreed to do so with the caveat that I might not be able to attend all committee meetings because of my flying duties with Delta. Notwithstanding that stipulation, I was able to arrange my flying schedule so I could attend both the board and the committee meetings. My attendance record and some comments made at the board meetings garnered Stanley's attention, and he reached out to me for lunch. This marked the beginning of a significant, long-term mentor/mentee association and warm relationship that lasted until Stanley passed at ninety-three years of age in 2013.

At that lunch, we discovered that we shared many common values and some common business interests, particularly in real estate development. Stanley had developed several large condominium projects, and I was currently converting a twelve-unit apartment building to condos on Beacon Hill. I was able to get his advice on that project and on another acquisition I was considering at the time.

As time passed, we became friendly outside of our American Cancer Society association and developed a much closer relationship. Through his influence and contacts, I was appointed to the board of a major financial institution in Boston that included very handsome directors' fees. He also invited me to participate as a junior partner in several large real estate ventures with his group of investors, and over time, I became a comanaging partner with him.

Stanley was also a great mentor during my volunteer years with the American Cancer Society. His wise counsel to me and influence in the state organization resulted in my eventually becoming chairman of the board of the Massachusetts division. Stanley went on to both serve on and chair the national board of the American Cancer Society. There is no doubt that my eventual service on the national board was directly due to the mentor relationship I was fortunate and humbled to have with a great instructor pilot, Stanley Shmishkiss.

HOW TO FIND YOUR INSTRUCTOR PILOTS

How do you find great instructor pilots (IPs) and develop mentor relationships that rocket you ahead?

1. Know why you want a mentor.
The first step is to be clear in your mind *why* you want a mentor and what you hope to gain from a relationship with that person. Be clear about what you need or want from your mentor and communicate that so the mentor knows how to help. Then listen to the advice that is given and don't be thin-skinned or defensive when you receive feedback that you may not want to hear.

TIP: Do not approach someone you may have admired from afar (but don't really know) to ask to be your mentor. It would probably be awkward for all concerned, especially if the person turns you down—which is likely what would happen. My suggestion is to start with someone you know and with whom you already have some sort of relationship.

2. Look in plain sight.
Your potential mentors may very well be hiding in plain sight—probably in a work setting. They are likely to be more senior people or individuals who are excelling in a given environment. You may also find potential mentors in your professional associations and in nonprofit organizations where you are volunteering. Having served on thirty boards, I have found, from both business and nonprofit arenas, that they are populated by a wide variety of people and often by significant leaders from the business and broader community.

continued

3. Find a mentoring program.

You may have a formalized mentoring program where you work. Many Fortune 500 companies have in-house sponsorship or mentoring programs that are run through their human resources department. Your alumni association is also a potential resource to explore. We set up a mentoring program to connect our graduates at the Association of Graduates of the Air Force Academy. It was online and voluntary, and a significant number of our graduates volunteered to be mentors for younger officers and others who had recently left the service and were transitioning to the business world.

4. Observe. Then give.

Your potential IP should be someone you've observed closely and possibly even studied. Based on your observations, you will have concluded that the person is someone you want to emulate or who has specific skill sets or qualities you would like to acquire. It is always best to give something before you ask to receive. Offer your mentor-to-be something: maybe tickets to a favorite event or an invitation to coffee or lunch.

5. Take a good look at yourself.

Take stock of yourself and ask whether you would want to mentor you. What kind of attitude do you display? What are you doing of note that will get you noticed or that sets you apart? Are you open-minded and easily coached? Are you humble, appreciative, and respectful of others? Bottom line: Why would someone want to spend time mentoring you?

6. Be committed to the process.

A great mentor relationship is usually a long-term affair. Follow through on your responsibilities and have the discipline to do what you say you will do. You want your mentors

> to feel that the time they are investing in you is worth it.
> Your credibility and follow-through are key to that end. My
> consistent follow-through on the advice given brought me
> many benefits.

I did well in Undergraduate Pilot Training and was all set to go off and become a Sierra Hotel (Sh*t Hot) fighter pilot. And while I did get to fly a fighter-type jet, my first Air Force pilot assignment was as an instructor pilot. It was my turn to become a mentor to young second lieutenants wanting to fly jets. I had come full circle in less than a year.

BECOME AN INSTRUCTOR PILOT

We can all use some help as we navigate through this thing called life. And as we make our own way, we can give some of ourselves to help others along their way. As we are being mentored, we can also mentor others. And even when you can't develop a deep mentoring relationship, taking the time to give some constructive criticism or to offer words of encouragement can sometimes have a remarkable effect. That's what the phrase "pay it forward" is all about. You'll see what I mean.

When I was a young copilot at Delta in 1985, I was flying a Tampa "turnaround" out of Atlanta. A turnaround means you fly in, drop off your passengers, board a new group of passengers, and fly back to your original location. Delta had renovated its terminal at Tampa, and this turnaround was my first flight in since it opened, so I decided to get off the airplane to check it out. I was going up an escalator when I spotted an African American guy in a shirt and tie coming down the other side. He was looking intently at me so I nodded a silent greeting.

When he got to the bottom, he jumped on the up escalator and chased me down. "Excuse me, sir, are you African American?"

I said, "Yes, absolutely."

"I thought so, but you may have been Puerto Rican or something else, so I didn't want to assume." Then he said, "My name is Jeff, and I just want to shake your hand because I have never met an African American airline pilot before." He went on to tell me that becoming an airline pilot had been his dream for years. He had flown small planes as much as he could, but he didn't have nearly enough flying time, and he knew that he was too old to achieve his dream. He was working in operations at the Tampa airport so he could be close to aviation.

I asked him how much flying time he had and how old he was. He said, "I have around 230 hours, and I'm thirty-four years old."

When Delta hired me, the average age of a new-hire pilot was about twenty-eight and a half. There was one guy in our class of twenty-four who was thirty years old, and we all wondered who he knew in corporate to have gotten hired. The airlines wanted to have pilots for a thirty-year career, and by federal law, the retirement age was sixty. It has since been increased to sixty-five. The minimum amount of flying time a candidate had to have to even be *considered* for an airline pilot position was 1,500 hours. The average flying time in my class was over 2,200 hours. So yes, Jeff was too old and lacking enough flying time to be eligible for a pilot's job, and of course, he knew that.

I felt there was no need to pile on by telling him what he already knew, so in the moment, I decided to take a different tack. "Jeff, every airline pilot I know had 230 hours at one time," I said.

"It's just a number on the way to building more time. And while thirty-four may be old today, who knows if that will be the case in five or ten years?" I encouraged him to keep flying as much as he could and to not give up on his dream.

Years later, after I became a captain, I was changing planes in the Cincinnati airport while flying a trip. This was back before everyone had cell phones, and I was on a pay phone checking in with my office in Boston. I could sense that someone was hovering close by. As I turned around, I saw a pilot who I thought was waiting to use the phone. He asked, "Captain Thompson?"

I said yes, wondering how he knew my name. But just before asking a dumb question, I realized I was wearing my name badge on my uniform. He said he wanted to reintroduce himself, because we had actually met once, thirteen years before in the Tampa airport—when he first saw me on the escalator. Having never forgotten that brief encounter, I immediately remembered who he was and I was happily surprised to see him in a pilot's uniform. He said he was flying a regional jet as a captain for Comair and went on to tell me how his journey had transpired.

Jeff said he had been looking for me in airports for years and had even reached out to Delta for my contact information. Because of employee privacy restrictions, the company was unable to help him. He said he had just wanted to thank me for being the only person who had not discouraged him from pursuing his dream by telling him he didn't have enough flying time or that he was too old. Because of my encouragement, he said, he had been inspired to chase his dream in a big way and was now living that dream every day.

During our first interaction that afternoon in Tampa, I was just being polite in a brief conversation, a passing social interaction.

But for Jeff, my decision to be positive was the seed for a whole new level of motivation to go after what he really wanted in life.

The lesson is simple but powerful. You never know how what you say or how you say it can affect another person's existence. The sway of positive interactions, whether through comments, advice, or a full mentoring relationship, can literally change a person's life. It's never too late to become someone's instructor pilot.

ENGAGING YOUR PASSENGERS

> *"My mother taught me that your*
> *employees come first. If you treat them*
> *well, then they treat the customers well,*
> *and that means your customers come*
> *back, and your shareholders are happy."*
>
> HERB KELLEHER,
> former CEO, Southwest Airlines

WHEN I WAS a captain at Delta, I often stood in the cockpit door and greeted the passengers as they boarded the plane. Then, after the flight was over, I thanked them for flying with us as they left. It was a small way to show my appreciation for their patronage (and for paying my salary). It also demonstrated, albeit in a short and fast way, the value of interacting with people—as occasionally, those short greetings led to further and often interesting conversations. The fact is you can find great value, in both a personal and professional way, in talking to and engaging with a wide variety of people on your Flight to Excellence.

In the current business lexicon, *engagement* is most often preceded by *employee*, and there can be no doubt that keeping your crew members engaged in the mission of the enterprise is critically important to the long-term success of the business. Research clearly substantiates that the more engaged your crew members are, the more successful your company will be.[6]

I watched and learned a great deal about the value of employee engagement during my years with Delta, which was founded on the principles of treating its employees as family and its customers with service, humility, and respect.

The secret to Delta's success is actually no secret at all. Delta's compensation has been industry leading, and it consistently appears as one of the best places to work, receiving high marks for its treatment of employees. It has not only been the most profitable airline in the world, but historically it has also shared those large profits with its employees in a plan that is considered among the best in any airline or blue-chip company. Because of its strong principles, the company's culture of loyalty from its crew members evidences itself in every aspect of the company's operation.

As a result of how it values, recognizes, and compensates its employees, Delta has developed a fiercely committed workforce that has a strong emotional connection to the company and a

---

6   Naz Beheshti, "10 Timely Statistics about the Connection between Employee Engagement and Wellness," *Forbes*, January 16, 2019, https://www.forbes.com/sites/nazbeheshti/2019/01/16/10-timely-statistics-about-the-connection-between-employee-engagement-and-wellness/#6e23199522a0.

dedication to the customers they serve. Delta's approach represents Employee Engagement 101, and I was proud to witness and be a part of that culture for over a quarter of a century.

PERSONAL ENGAGEMENT: GETTING IN

Engagement is also an important communication skill, and on an individual level, it can be a critical asset in business and personal success. An engaged conversationalist possesses an essential leadership talent. Mastering that skill will likely enable you to communicate your vision, plans, and direction in an inspiring, motivating, and confident way. People will feel comfortable around you and will enjoy being in your presence. In this age of tweeting, texting, and email, being a good conversationalist can set you apart from your contemporaries and create a lasting positive impression. Research has also shown that talking with others has a positive effect on your health, creates happiness, and contributes to greater longevity.

Some people have the gift of gab and are naturally engaging. They're the life of the party. They know what to say, how to say it, and when to say it for maximum effect. But many of us find engaging in conversations uncomfortable at best; others find it often difficult and maybe even intimidating. Some of us may just be naturally shy (or an introvert on the DISC scale).[7]

The good news is that by using a fairly simple process, you can become better at engaging people, and the rewards are frequently interesting and often valuable conversations (as they were for me

7   DISC is a behavior assessment tool based on the DISC theory of psychologist William Moulton Marston, which centers on four different personality traits: Dominance (D), Influence (I), Steadiness (S), and Conscientiousness (C). This theory was then developed into a behavioral assessment tool by industrial psychologist Walter Vernon Clarke.

when I greeted the passengers before and after a flight). And as with most things in life, you can practice and get better as you hone your talent.

I recommend the following ten steps if you want to become better at engaging people and building your conversation skills.

1. BUILD YOUR CONFIDENCE

If you are naturally shy, practice engaging random people with harmless small talk. Start with people you know and feel comfortable with. Then expand the circle of contact with others in everyday situations like colleagues at work, the cashier at the grocery store, or people you see often at your gym. Make it a habit by continuing to engage on a regular basis. In relatively short order, you'll begin to become comfortable engaging people, and it will be your new paradigm.

2. BECOME A BETTER LISTENER

Ironically, becoming a better listener will help make you a better conversationalist. Listening to someone else takes more effort than speaking does. It is easy to get distracted when we are listening, and we naturally want to talk—and we usually want to talk about ourselves. Here's a tip you can use as your secret weapon to engage others: *Elicit information from people to get them talking about themselves.* They'll feel complimented when you want to know more about them, and most people will warmly open up in conversation.

3. BE GENUINELY INTERESTED

Have a true desire to get to know the person you are talking to. The normal, everyday questions we ask upon meeting someone new are always a good start: *What do you do? Where do you live? Do you have kids? Tell me about them.* The answers to these questions can take the conversation down a number of different roads. And all you have to do is listen.

4. MAKE AND MAINTAIN EYE CONTACT

Making eye contact is a key action to remember, particularly with the ubiquity of cell phone use today. No one will feel that you are truly engaged if you keep glancing at your cell phone every few seconds. The same is true if you are constantly scanning the room looking for someone who may be more interesting or important to talk to, which comes across as being disrespectful and rude. Keeping eye contact shows that you are giving your full attention to the person you are with and to the conversation you are sharing.

5. TAKE THE TIME TO DEVELOP GOOD QUESTIONS

Most people will ask the same typical question when they first greet someone: "How are you doing?" You can anticipate the usual answer: "Fine." With that one-word answer, the conversation is already set to die. But taking the time to choose a more open-ended question can truly engage someone and keep your conversation rolling. I usually ask, "So tell me, what's new and exciting in your life?" This question can get someone thinking and talking about what may actually be going on in their life or something they are excited about in the future. Then often they'll ask me the same question back, which gives me the opportunity to respond in a unique way. At that point, the conversation has any number of promising directions and topics.

"So tell me, what's new and
exciting in your life?"

6. BE GENEROUS WITH PRAISE

We all like to receive compliments. A compliment tells us that someone has noticed and valued something positive about us and taken the effort to communicate that in a favorable way. Receiving a compliment makes you feel good about yourself and also gives you a positive disposition toward the person who complimented you. On the flip side, giving praise also benefits you. Research shows that the giver of a compliment also receives a positive psychological boost in their mood and temperament, so everybody wins. A note of caution: A compliment must be genuine. False praise will be seen for what it is. And it's important to remember that a compliment should not be inappropriate from either a setting or from a gender perspective. You don't want to say, "You look good for your age."

7. DIG DEEPER

The usual small talk containing everyday pleasantries is perfectly fine, but often the deeper the level of the conversation goes, the greater the rewards you'll see from it. These can be intellectual or tangible rewards. Of course, you'll need the appropriate "charts" in your flight kit to be able to uphold a certain level of discourse. That is to say, you'll want to be up on current events and issues in politics, sports, and other news. It also helps conversation if you have a certain in-depth knowledge about an interesting topic that others may not be that familiar with. The chances of having a memorable conversation increase dramatically when you go to a level that is more substantial and outside the norm.

8. BE ENTERTAINING

You want your conversations to be entertaining and engaging, not dull and boring. Don't be afraid to tell a good joke or share a humorous story. Show your communication partners that you have a lighthearted side. Feel free to smile, laugh, or use other facial expressions or hand gestures to make your points. Adding a little excitement and fun will help you have a conversation both parties will want to remember and talk about.

9. SHOW RESPECT

One of my biggest pet peeves is when someone interrupts another person before that person has completed stating their thoughts. This is simply impolite; there's no other way to describe it, and it indicates a lack of respect for the other person. Yes, you may want to make your point or correct something you feel is incorrect or just plain wrong. But please, please, please, wait your turn! The least it will do is break the other person's train of thought; the most it will do is mark you as someone with bad manners.

10. BE YOURSELF

Finally, don't put on airs or try to be something or someone you're not. Be honest about your feelings, but always do so in a respectful way. You don't always have to agree on what is being discussed, and at times you may have a difference of opinion with those you are in conversation with. But above all, be respectful of your partner's viewpoint—even if ultimately you'll just have to agree to disagree.

PERSONAL ENGAGEMENT: GETTING OUT

These ten steps should help you become better at engaging others, but they don't cover every situation. At times, you may not be in the mood to be an engaging conversationalist, or you just don't want to be bothered. Or you may be in a conversation that you would really like to end. I've been there, and I'm sure you have too.

The issue then becomes how to extricate yourself from the conversation. This topic is common enough that you can find numerous articles and even some books on the subject. I have found that if I am in a group setting and I can leave with little notice, I simply excuse myself and just quietly leave. If you are part of a smaller conversation, you can ask for a business card or offer yours. This is a clear and universal signal that the conversation is ending. In fact, simply excusing yourself is just fine and all that is necessary. Most people will assume that you are going to the restroom or have something else pressing to do and won't question why you need to be excused. The bottom line is that if you are focused but polite and respectful, you can be on your way without making too much of an issue about it.

THE BENEFITS

The right chat with the right person can be informative and educational, and can substantially build your knowledge base. It can also result in immediate or tangible longer-term benefits, as the following story reveals.

I was "deadheading" on a flight from Boston to New York City so that I could fly a plane from New York down to Atlanta. (Deadheading means you are on duty and in uniform, but you are riding in the cabin. The airline is repositioning you from one city to another so you can pick up a flight somewhere else or sometimes begin a layover break.) As I took my seat in first class, the gentleman in the seat next to me made a joking comment. "Shouldn't you be in the cockpit?" I laughed and explained that I was deadheading and what that meant. Deadheading was the opening for a conversation that eventually got me into a new business venture that would become a sizable part of my company.

After I had settled into my seat, my seatmate and I chatted a bit about where I was headed that day for Delta. After talking about the airline business from a pilot's perspective, I asked him what line of business he was in. He explained that he was the CEO of a firm that consulted in the food service industry and that his company had just completed an assignment with PepsiCo. We joked about Delta's strong relationship with Coke, how both dominated business in Atlanta, and how Pepsi would never find its way onto a Delta jet.

PepsiCo at the time, in addition to its beverage lines, was also a major player in the food service industry. The company owned Frito-Lay, Taco Bell, Pizza Hut, and Kentucky Fried Chicken. The work he had just completed centered on the Pizza Hut division, and he had just made his concluding report to the division CEO.

As we chatted, I mentioned that I was also an attorney and business owner. I shared that I had considered becoming a fast-food franchisee but had not taken steps as yet to pursue that line of business.

My new conversation partner became much more engaged as he began to politely ask more probing questions about my business ventures. The more we talked, the more interested he became, before finally proclaiming, "You would be a great Pizza Hut franchisee!" He went on to tell me that the company was actively looking for qualified minority businesspeople who had both the investment capital and business savvy to become Pizza Hut franchisees, and he felt I would be a prime candidate. He pulled out one of his business cards, wrote a name and number on the back, and handed it to me. He said, "This is the president of Pizza Hut, and this is his direct line. Give him a call and tell him that I suggested he talk to you. I'm sure you'll have an interesting conversation." Just then, the captain came on the microphone and said, "We've been cleared to land."

The flight from Boston to New York is a relatively short one, and our conversation seemed to have barely gotten started before it was time to disembark and head our different ways. Yet in less than an hour, I had engaged in an interesting conversation, learned some fascinating information on the fast-food business, gotten an inside look at some of the issues facing a major corporation, and made a valuable contact in that business.

THE REST OF THE STORY

I did make the call to the number on the card and had an interesting conversation with the president of Pizza Hut. Based on some of the work that my new friend had done for them, they were revamping their franchise program and expected it to be done in about eight months. He invited me to keep in touch as they went through this process. I called my new friend to let him know that I had followed up and to apprise him of Pizza Hut's current situation. I thanked him again for an engaging conversation and the great contact with Pizza Hut.

Well, he had another client contact! He told me he was doing some work with a fast-growing outfit "up my way" called Subway. He gave me the number of his associate at Subway corporate, and after a phone call, I was invited down to Milford, Connecticut, to meet with them and to tour their new corporate world headquarters. By chance on the tour, I met Subway's founder, Fred DeLuca, and after a brief conversation, he offered to take me on the rest of the tour. I subsequently became the first Subway franchisee in the city of Boston. My company, Summit Food Services, went on to become a multi-unit, multi-brand fast-food company with Subway, Dunkin' Donuts, and TCBY operations. And all of that evolved from a short, humorous line: "Shouldn't you be in the cockpit?"

YOU CAN BECOME ENGAGING

Many people find it very difficult to engage and speak with people in a public setting. Research into public speaking shows why this is a very common fear for a significant part of the population.[8]

continued

---

8   Theo Tsaousides, "Why Are We Scared of Public Speaking?" *Psychology Today*, November 27, 2017, https://www.psychologytoday.com/us/blog/smashing-the-brainblocks/201711/why-are-we-scared-public-speaking.

But that fear is only a part of a larger problem called social anxiety, which is said to affect more than 20 million people. Many of these people find it difficult to even interact with others because of deep-seated fears about being rejected, embarrassed, or judged.

While I've never had social anxiety, I can appreciate how someone suffering from that condition might feel, because I was a very shy person for a great part of my younger years. Although I'm not a psychoanalyst, I believe my shyness was a combination of a natural tendency coupled with being in a series of environments that, over time, made it very comfortable to be introverted and alone.

I went to Catholic schools during my elementary and middle school years, when the nuns were very strict and talking to a classmate was considered "disrupting" the class. My high school years were spent integrating an all-white high school in the Deep South. With only a small group of black kids at the school and with the majority of the white kids hostile to our presence, it was more comfortable to stay to myself as much as possible.

At the Air Force Academy, we were taught teamwork and leadership, but for the entire first year, anytime you were out of your dorm room, you weren't allowed to speak to your classmates at all or to an upperclassman unless spoken to. Being out of your room was akin to being in the "jungle." You kept your head down and hoped not to get confronted by one of the upperclass "predators."

Even my early years as an Air Force pilot were fairly isolated. I was often the only African American pilot in my flying squadron, and as an instructor pilot flying a fighter-type jet, my only other crew member was a student navigator or pilot. And in our program, we had a different student for each flight.

But some enlisted airmen began to engage me. It was

usually an older African American sergeant who would come up and salute me before telling me how proud he was to see those silver wings on my chest. Quite honestly, I found it uncomfortable at first, but I began to feel more at ease as I crafted a response that was modest and appreciative while still honoring the officer-enlisted decorum. It wasn't until I was promoted to a leadership job with thirty-five enlisted airmen and civilians reporting to me that I felt obligated to totally come out of the shyness shell.

As time passed, overcoming shyness became something that I paid attention to and worked to be better at. The more effort I put in, the better I became. I'll also confess that I had a strong underlying personal motivation. Having those African American sergeants, who were always older than me, express pride in me created a sense of obligation and responsibility. I never wanted to be perceived as arrogant, egotistical, or unappreciative of their respect. Yet I was operating in a military environment, and I was the young boss. I had to work at being engaging and setting the right tone while still adhering to the proper protocols.

The situation was even more pronounced when I went to the airlines. With the African American pilot population at Delta less than 1 percent over the course of my entire career, it was a rarity for other Delta employees to see a black pilot. With ever greater regularity, my African American colleagues who worked in other areas at Delta expressed their pride in having me at the company. I felt the same sense of responsibility with them that I felt with those older Air Force sergeants. I was very intentional in pleasantly engaging them, and soon it became my habit. It was second nature and no longer the uncomfortable feeling it had been just a few years before.

My point is that for most people, being engaging doesn't

continued

come naturally. And for millions, it is actually a major challenge in life. But it's a skill that can be learned and mastered and will ultimately add to your communication, social, and leadership skills. It's the secret weapon that helps us connect in business, politics, and even with family and friends. When you become good at it, people will open up to you and doors may even open for greater opportunities in your life.

REACH OUT

Like many people, I'm not naturally good at remembering names. (But in spite of not being naturally skilled at names, I have managed to actually become good at it, by making some type of immediate association.) Having that skill has increased people's perception of me as an engaging person. It has also brought me small, unexpected favors that help to make daily life a little nicer.

During my military years, we all wore our names on our chest. On some of the uniforms, my name was permanently sewed onto the jacket or shirt. Other uniforms required a separate name tag to be attached. I never gave either one of them much thought, as it was just a small part of how we operated in the armed services—though it did make it easier to identify someone if you needed to.

For some positions in the airline business, the requirement is the same. Pilots at Delta are required to wear name tags on their shirts and uniform coats. Flight attendants, gate agents, and ticket counter agents are required to wear their names on their uniforms as well. It was in this setting that I began to notice and use my colleagues' names when I spoke to them, sometimes with pleasantly surprising results.

It all began on the airplane with the flight attendants. I made it a point to introduce myself and to call them by their names, which made the short time we had together in an often fast-paced work environment much easier to endure. Just that small act often produced a smile and occasionally a nice first-class meal on the flight.

I also began to notice that many other people wear their names in a business or professional setting as either a part of their uniforms or with the addition of a name tag. The list is quite long: employees at the fast-food restaurant, the customer service representative at the bank, and the cashier at the grocery store. There's the hotel representative when I check in and the rental car agent when I get my car. My doctor even has his name stitched on his white coat.

It has become my habit to use a name if I see it displayed. As with the flight attendants, it generally produces a smile and sometimes a surprised look. One young lady was shocked that I called her by her name and asked me how I knew her. She worked in the Au Bon Pain restaurant at the Cincinnati airport, where I usually grabbed a sandwich and a chocolate chip cookie while changing flights. Joking, I told her that I was disappointed she didn't remember when we previously met and the great conversation we had. As she racked her brain trying to remember, I fessed up and reminded her that she had her name tag on her shirt. We both laughed as she told me that no customers had ever called her by her name before.

We became friendly, as she would often be working as I passed through Cincy and got my sandwich and cookie. She even began to give me the cookie at no charge. When I thanked her but politely refused the cookie for free, she insisted, saying, "We'll have leftovers that we throw away anyway." I often wondered how many cookies my Subway employees were "throwing away" to customers because they had used their names!

During my tenure as president and CEO of the Association of Graduates at the Air Force Academy, I was issued an identification badge that gave me access through the employee gate at the base. As you approached the gate in your car, you would come to a complete stop and give the military policeman your ID to be checked before being allowed to continue. The police changed positions at the gate quite frequently, so there was little chance to get to know them personally. I always greeted them with a smile (using their names, which were displayed on their uniform) and wished them a nice day.

I had just finished a workout at the base gym one day when my executive assistant called to ask where I was. She had put a meeting on my schedule with a retired general but had forgotten to let me know. I told her I was leaving the gym and would be there in five minutes. As I sped back to my office, I saw the blue lights in my rearview mirror and knew that I had a steep ticket coming my way. As I pulled over to take my medicine, the policeman pulled up next to my car. He said, "Slow it down a little, Mr. Thompson." And then he drove on off.

I didn't know the policeman, and with over 10,000 people at the Academy, I don't know how he knew my name. My guess was that he was on duty at the entrance gate one day and I greeted him using his name. Perhaps as a result, he made note of my name from my ID. In any event, it saved me a very expensive ticket that day.

I'm not an expert in communication, nor do I claim to be a great conversationalist. But over the years I have noticed, experienced, and come to appreciate the value that being an engaging person can have on someone's life. While I've mentioned a few of the tangible benefits, there are many intangible benefits as well: As you work on engaging with people, you will find that you are also overcoming fear, building self-confidence, relieving stress, and developing charisma. Interesting conversations, a different level of knowledge, novel experiences, and even the opening of a new world are possible when you are primed to reach out and engage others.

=PART III=

YOUR
FLIGHT
PLAN

*"Having a plan enabled us
to keep our hope alive."*

—CHELSEA "SULLY" SULLENBERGER,
airline captain and "Hero of the Hudson,"
Air Force Academy Class of 1973

DEFINING YOUR VISION
AND YOUR DESTINATION

*"Vision is a destination—a fixed point
to which we focus all effort."*

–SIMON SINEK,
British-born American author
and motivational speaker

I WAS DOWN in my basement recently, rummaging through old flight records. My mission was to see how much flying time I had accumulated over the years. As I leafed through my logbooks, the names of some of the more exotic and exciting places I had flown to brought back fond and heartwarming memories. I miss those days. But I digress. Back to my mission: total flying time. When I added airline flying, military flying time, and personal civilian flying time all together, I calculated that I had over 18,500 hours—18,773 hours to be exact—of being up in the air. Let's do a little math to put that number in perspective.

If we divide my total flying time by 24, the number of hours in a day, we get 782 total days up in the air. For a different viewpoint, we can divide the 782 days by 30, the average number of days in a month, and we arrive at 26 overall months speeding through the sky. Or finally, by converting the 18,773 hours to years brings us to two years and two months of being off the earth and booming up in the blue. Any way you slice it, that's a lot of time off terra firma.

With that backdrop, let me share with you one plain, remarkable fact. *Never, ever*—not even once—in 18,773 hours, 782 days, 26 months (or over two years and two months), did I take off without knowing exactly where I planned to land.

Well, to be honest, there were a few times, because of weather, mechanical problems, or other changes in circumstances, that I *ended up* somewhere other than where I had planned. But those occasions were the exception to the rule, and my original statement is still true. I always took off knowing where I *planned* to land.

Most military and civilian airline flights are required to operate with a flight plan that specifically details the particulars of that individual flight. These flight plans state where the flight will originate, what departure procedure will be used, the jetway or airway routes that are expected to be taken, and the arrival procedure to be used at the stated destination. In fact, when a plane is about 100 miles away from the airport, as the pilot you'll also be assigned the specific runway that you can expect to land on.

What I am trying to stress here is that in professional aviation, you need to be very clear and definite about where you are headed and how you expect to get there well before you ever take off. It only makes sense that from the very start, you have your destination clearly defined. When you are in the cockpit of a jet flying at 40,000 feet and at 600 miles per hour, you don't have the option of pulling off on the side of the road to try to figure it out.

> *"If you don't know where you're going,*
> *how can you ever expect to arrive?"*

Likewise in life, if you want to get to a lofty place, you'll need to have a very clear vision of where you want to go and how you expect to get there. After all, if you don't know where you're going, how can you ever expect to arrive?

THE FLIGHT THROUGH LIFE

Your vision, quite simply, is your destination specifically defined. Let me pause here and emphasize that it needs to be your vision and not someone else's vision for you. It has to be your passion, your hunger, and your desire, with a strong sense of clarity for what you want. A few questions will illustrate why specificity is so crucially important.

Suppose you grew up on the East Coast of the United States and had always wanted to visit and experience the West Coast. You now have the time and money to take that often dreamed-of jaunt. In planning your trip, would you go to the airline counter and ask to buy a ticket to "the West Coast"? How about buying a ticket to California? That wouldn't quite do it either. You would need to tell the ticket agent the name of a specific city in California. And you would need to tell her the specific date that you would want to travel, as well as the time of day. She would also want to know what part of the airplane you would want to fly in—first class or coach. And she would ask you whether you preferred a window seat or an aisle. You get my point. You have to know exactly where and how you want to go if you ever expect to get there.

Most people generally understand this concept when it comes to travel. Why, then, do they find it so difficult to apply this same methodology to create a vision for their flight through life?

Many folks have never gone through the process of defining their true vision because they don't know what they really want. We may sometimes have a vague notion of what we might be able to do with our lives or what path we may be able to take, but defining a true-life vision requires much more. It requires a certainty of purpose, which creates the passion to achieve your desired goal.

For a good part of my childhood years, my mom and dad were both schoolteachers. It was a profession that seemed to run in the family, at least on my father's side. He had three brothers and a sister, and they all, and some of their spouses, taught school for either a significant part of their adult lives or their entire careers. For quite some time, I never gave much thought to what I would do professionally when I grew up. Lying dormant in the back of my mind was the assumption that I would probably be a schoolteacher one day like my parents. That is, until the day I decided I wouldn't.

I had not had a good day at school the afternoon it happened. But on that day, my life was changed forever. It's still not easy for me to adequately describe how I felt at that moment. But I will try my best to relate what happened so that perhaps you can see some of what I saw or hear some of what I heard so you can feel, vicariously, the emotion I felt.

I was walking home from school, and I was feeling a little

down. It had been a particularly tough day for me at Orangeburg High. As I walked along a dirt road with my shoulders slumped and my head hanging down, all of a sudden and literally out of the blue, I was engulfed by a large shadow and a roar from above. For a brief moment, the sun disappeared.

As I raised my head in shock to see what was happening, the ground started to shake. A blast of air almost knocked me over, and the roar became deafening. A sleek Air Force fighter jet flew right over my head! The plane was so low I could actually smell the gas fumes and feel the heat from the engines on my face. My first thought was that the plane was about to crash.

I froze as I stood watching it. The jet was heading lower and lower toward the ground, but at what seemed to be the last second, the pilot pulled the plane's nose straight up toward the sky and began to roll it around and around.[9]

It was a bright spring afternoon, and the sun's reflection off that sleek, silver body almost blinded me. I then heard a loud *boom*, and a stream of fire came out of the tail as the pilot kicked that jet into afterburner, and it almost instantly disappeared into that clear blue sky.

I stood in that spot, transfixed and speechless, with my mouth gaping open. I had never been in an airplane. In fact, I had never even seen one up close on the ground. Being a witness to such a rare phenomenon right before my eyes was the most exciting and exhilarating thing I had ever experienced. I didn't realize it at the time, but the seed of my dream to one day fly jets was planted that very afternoon.

---

9 An aircraft in flight is free to rotate in three dimensions: yaw—nose left or right about an axis running up and down; pitch—nose up or down about an axis running from wing to wing; and roll—rotation about an axis running from nose to tail.

For the next several days, I couldn't get the sight of that jet and the totality of what I had experienced out of my mind. And then—almost as an afterthought—I realized that someone had actually been inside that flying machine, making it do the wondrous things that I had seen. My fascination with what I had seen shifted to wondering about how someone got to do something so exciting. That was the impetus that moved me to start exploring the process of becoming a pilot.

There was no internet back then, so the main depository of information was the school library. I began to trek to the library during my study hall periods so I could read books or magazine articles about aviation. The more I read and learned, the more excited I became. Over time, I began to discover some of the various paths to becoming a professional pilot, and I realized that becoming a pilot was something I could possibly do. I was subtly embracing the idea of becoming an Air Force pilot, and gradually and steadily that idea was becoming my personal vision in life.

Ironically, the more I learned about becoming a pilot and the more I realized it was something I had the ability to do, the more I also faced a painful truth. As a young African American kid in the segregated South, I was a million miles away from achieving that vision.

Yet I couldn't denounce the principles my parents had constantly instilled in me: With hard work, dedication, and determination, I could accomplish anything I put my mind to. Embracing their words, I fought off the self-doubt and committed myself to going all out to achieve my vision—despite the challenges of my external circumstances. I made the determined decision that I was going to fly for the US Air Force.

CREATING THE VISION

Experiencing that magnificent jet flying over me on that spring afternoon gave birth to my vision. It was a rare and unique occurrence, and many people may not have an extraordinary event to inspire them to pursue their vision like I did. What, then, is essential to move you to create an amazing vision that stirs your passion? The process has to begin with deep and resolute thought, and *thinking* is often the most difficult thing to achieve.

For most people, *doing* is much easier than thinking, since it does occupy the majority of our time. The problem is that most of what we *do* is not focused on accomplishing a vision that supports achieving excellence in our lives. Endless busyness and time spent on unimportant tasks inevitably get in the way of the thinking that is required to create a vision worthy of who we can truly become.

How do you break out of what can be a downward spiral of mediocre *doing*? How do you rocket to a high-level vision rooted in excellence and designed to enable you to achieve more in life? By entering a holding pattern and taking the time to think and answer some fundamental questions that will provide you with a vector to a better and more fulfilling life.

THE SKY'S THE LIMIT

You can begin this thought process by asking yourself this: What would you do with your life if there were no ceilings or any other limitations on you? What if money was no object, and you were guaranteed not to crash and burn? What would you find truly enjoyable and fulfilling to do? The world is full of people who are stuck in an unfulfilling career because it pays the bills; it is critically important that you look to the future and have a clear vision about where you want to be—rather than just accepting a career or job simply because you are capable of doing it or because it seems like the easiest path you can take at the time.

As you begin the process of thinking deeply about your vision, focus on the things you currently love doing or the things that, given the chance, you would give almost anything to do. Give effort and concentration to the things that are truly important to you and that matter most in your life. A clear vision is always in concert with your guiding principles and reflective of the values you hold dear.

> ➤ Follow the Air Force slogan "Aim High" as you go through the process. Why drive a bus if you can fly a jet?

> ➤ Be inventive and creative, and don't impose limitations on yourself.

> ➤ It costs nothing to think big.

> ➤ Using your imagination is free.

Creating a vision that you are passionate about and committed to will be tremendously fulfilling for who you are. Your ultimate goal is to figure out what you really want to do with your life and then put yourself in a position to actually get it done.

A HERO'S VISION

Some years ago, I attended a luncheon at a restaurant on Boston Harbor sponsored by a statewide aviation group. The guest speaker was one of my true living flying heroes, so I had made it a priority to attend. There was a small VIP reception prior to the main event, and as commissioner of aeronautics for Massachusetts, I was invited to attend.

My hero, Chuck Yeager, was as impressive as I could have imagined: humble and down-to-earth, yet pleasant and engaging. We had a short but enjoyable conversation, and he asked for two of my Delta pilot business cards. To my surprise, he was kind enough to later send one of those business cards back to me. It was autographed and accompanied by a copy of his autobiographical book, *Yeager*. He was a pilot's pilot and every bit deserving of his immortal place in aeronautical history.

THE FASTEST MAN ALIVE

As a young boy, Charles E. "Chuck" Yeager lived in one of the poorest counties in West Virginia, although he would tell you that he never felt poor. He grew up in a close-knit family with a hardworking mom and dad. They instilled strong moral values in their children and taught them by setting good examples. His dad worked as a natural-gas driller and was away from the family for five days a week, but always devoted himself on the weekends to spending time with his kids. He taught his boys how to live off the land, and young Yeager became a skilled hunter and fisherman like his dad.

Although his mom was the one who primarily raised him and his four siblings, Yeager says he took more after his dad. His father instilled in him a strong belief in the pursuit of excellence and required that he always do his very best. It was a condition that came naturally to young Yeager and an obligation that he readily adopted. From his 1985 autobiography, Yeager states, "Like Dad, I had certain standards that

continued

I lived by. Whatever I did, I determined to do the best I could at it. I was prideful about keeping my word and finishing what I started. That's how I was raised."

His dad was a gifted mechanic, and young Yeager also developed an avid interest in how things worked. He loved to fix things and found it a joy to tinker with his dad's old truck. After graduating from high school, he enlisted in the Army Air Corps and trained as an aircraft mechanic in the midst of World War II. Shortly thereafter, under a "flying sergeants" program, he trained to become a pilot and knew that he had found his passion in life.

Yeager loved to fly and did so more than anyone else in his squadron. His vision was to be the top pilot in the unit, and he worked hard to achieve that goal. Competitive by nature, he was driven to excel, to be the best in anything he did. He finished at the top of his class with that vision achieved. He trained as a fighter pilot flying the P-51 Mustang and was transferred to the European theater of the war.

Shot down after flying only eight missions, Yeager had to escape from France through the Pyrenees Mountains into Spain. The rule was, if you were a successful evadee, you couldn't fly again and would be shipped back Stateside. This rule was in place to protect the French Underground, which was helping our downed pilots escape. The fear was that if you were subsequently shot down again and captured by the Germans, you would be able to provide them with valuable information on the Underground. But he would have none of it. "I was raised to finish what I started, not slink off after flying only eight missions. Screw the regulation. I was brassy and pushed my way up the chain of command . . . arguing my case," Yeager states in his autobiography.

He petitioned and received an audience with General Dwight D. "Ike" Eisenhower, the Supreme Allied Commander, and Yeager made his case to fly again. To his surprise and that of many others, Ike gave the order to allow him to return to combat flying. On October 12, 1944, while escorting American B-24 bombers over Holland, he shot down five German fighters, becoming America's first "ace in a day." The headline in *Stars and Stripes* blared, "FIVE KILLS VINDICATES IKE'S DECISION!" Yeager's reputation as a top-gun fighter pilot was launched. He would finish the war with eleven and a half kills,[10] returning home as a hero.

Once back in the States, he married his wartime sweetheart, Glennis, who he had met during his initial flight training in California before shipping off to war. His new assignment was as a test pilot at Wright Field in Ohio. With the vision of becoming the best test pilot ever, he flew just about every plane on the base. He quickly earned the reputation of being the best of the best at Wright Field, and because of his superior flight performance, Yeager was selected to fly in air shows around the country.

He was next transferred to Muroc Army Base (which would become Edwards Air Force Base) in California in the fall of 1945, and his timing was perfect. The Air Corps was transitioning from propeller planes to jets, and he got to fly the newest and fastest planes ever built. It was here that he would truly earn his fame.

At Muroc, the Bell Aircraft Company was testing a spectacular new aircraft, the Bell X-1 that had been designed to break the sound barrier. No airplane had ever achieved this feat, and many engineers theorized that a physical barrier existed that would cause an airplane to disintegrate in the sky as it approached this limit. This imagined "brick wall," they speculated, is what prevented flight beyond the speed of sound.

continued

---

10 On occasion, two pilots might both be shooting at the same enemy aircraft, which gets destroyed. They would both be credited with half a kill.

The initial tests were successful, but as the Bell team got closer to approaching Mach 1, the actual speed of sound, the civilian test pilot, Chalmers "Slick" Goodlin, demanded a $150,000 bonus (about $1.8 million in today's dollars) for the danger of taking the X-1 through Mach 1. The entire project was stuck while Bell negotiated with Goodlin to resolve the pay issue. The Army Air Corps recognized the unlimited potential the X-1 program would have for future military application and took over the program.

Yeager threw his hat in the ring to become the pilot for the program but figured his chances of being selected were slim. He was just a high school graduate and would be competing with other test pilots who were college graduates with much more engineering education and experience. Because of his reputation for pursuing excellence, which had resulted in his superior flying skills, coupled with his natural mechanic's interest in learning everything about the planes he flew, he was chosen to fly the top secret Bell X-1.

Yeager became a member of an extraordinary team of scientists and engineers from the National Advisory Committee for Aeronautics, which was the forerunner to NASA. The project engineer for the X-1 was a Caltech aeronautical engineer named Jack Ridley. An excellent test pilot in his own right, Ridley made technical contributions to the team that were invaluable to its success. "I trusted Jack with my life," Yeager said. "I had a great deal of confidence in him and, you know, if he said something, that, to me, was from the Bible. You could take it to the bank."

As Yeager began flying the jet, the X-1 team enjoyed steady success. He was able to increase the speed of the plane from .8 to .9 Mach. But when he approached the speed of sound, the aircraft began a violent buffet, and the pitch controls froze. It seemed that the engineers who had predicted the "brick wall" scenario were right.

But with some engineering modifications by Ridley to the airplane's tail, the record-setting run seemed ready to be pursued.

The night before the flight, Chuck and Glennis went horseback riding in the desert. Racing back to the stables in the dark, he failed to see that the gate was closed and he was thrown from his horse, cracking two of his ribs. Knowing that his commanding officer would not let him fly with his injuries, he went to a civilian doctor off base who wrapped his ribs. He knew that despite his injuries, he would be able to fly the jet on that trial mission the next day.

The date was October 14, 1947, when he climbed again into the Bell X-1. As he lit the rockets and the speed increased toward Mach 1, the aircraft remained stable. The engineering modifications implemented by Ridley had worked. At .965 Mach, the speed jumped off the scale and an explosion was heard on the ground. Many thought the X-1 had exploded in the air and that Yeager had finally "bought the farm." In fact, it was the first sonic boom ever heard on Earth. Chuck Yeager had bored a hole in the sky, breaking the sound barrier and becoming the fastest man alive.

Chuck Yeager was a man with a vision and a clearly defined destination. But flying faster than the speed of sound was not his destination; it was just a stop on the Flight to Excellence and to being the best pilot he could be. He didn't do it for the money or to become famous. He did it because it was his duty and his passion. When asked what he was thinking when he broke the sound barrier, his response was classically simple: "Just doing my job."

Of course, fame and fortune followed. Yeager would go on to break other flight records and receive numerous awards from a host of organizations and institutions, including Congress and the president of the United States. He would grace the cover of *Time* magazine, eventually earn the rank of brigadier general in the Air Force, and become a multimillionaire, ultimately earning the unofficial title of "the greatest pilot of all time."

Chuck Yeager has lived life to the fullest and was privileged to experience things that most people would have trouble even dreaming about. Yet he has always appreciated the life he has been given and has been true to the guiding principles he learned as a young boy from his mom and dad. As quoted in a *Huntington Quarterly* magazine article entitled "Yeager: The Best There Ever Was," he stated:

> I've had a full life and enjoyed just about every damned minute of it, because that's how I lived. My beginnings back in West Virginia tell who I am to this day. My accomplishments as a pilot tell more about luck, happenstance, and a person's destiny. But the guy who broke the sound barrier was the kid who swam the Mud River with a swiped watermelon, or shot the head off a squirrel before school.

The Chuck Yeager story shows that deep inside every one of us, there is more than many of us ever imagine. Our circumstances ultimately don't determine what we can accomplish in life. It didn't matter that he was from the backwoods of West Virginia. It didn't matter that his family was considered poor. It didn't matter that his dad was gone for five days every week. And it didn't matter that he only had a high school education.

What did matter were the bedrock principles that he lived by, rooted in integrity and inspired by his mom and dad. It mattered that he had a plan to become a top-gun fighter pilot, which carried over into his test pilot career. It also mattered that he was surrounded by talented and dedicated people who, like him, were committed to performing at the highest levels. It mattered that Yeager was flying the P4 System to success and that he was devoted to a life of excellence and being the very best that he could be.

John H. Houvouras, editor of the *Huntington Quarterly*, summed it up best in that 1998 article about Yeager, saying,

> Although his legend looms larger than life, he has never forgotten his roots or relented in his pursuit of being the best. And everyone, at some point in their life, has longed to be the best at something. Everyone, at one time or another, has dreamt of living life to the fullest. Chuck Yeager, the hillbilly from West Virginia who flew like a demon and never backed down from a challenge, epitomizes that hunger in all of us.

YOUR MISSION:
THE WAY FORWARD

*"Remain focused on fulfilling your
business mission. Never allow adversity
to divert your attention and efforts."*

–RICHARD BRANSON,
British business magnate,
founder of Virgin Airlines

OUR VISION IS where we want to go. Our mission is what
we need to do to get there.

Mission planning is the process of developing the strategy that
gets you to your destination. Forming a plan is a basic requirement for any trip you take. It can be a short trip to see a friend
or a vacation halfway around the world. Granted, the short trips

may almost seem intuitive, but the planning process, even if done unconsciously, still takes place. The characteristics and complexities of your vision determine what the mission-planning process will be. Let's continue to use the flight analogy to succinctly illustrate the point.

If the origination point of your flight is Atlanta and your destination (vision) is Savannah, then your mission planning will be relatively simple. It is a fairly short flight, less than an hour of airtime, so the fuel required will not present either a takeoff-weight or detailed planning issue. The weather patterns will most likely be similar because both cities are in Georgia. Passenger amenity issues such as food service or other comforts are negligible because of the short duration of the flight, and if you have a serious emergency, you will either turn back and go to Atlanta or just proceed on to Savannah.

If, however, your destination is San Francisco, your mission will require much more detailed and complicated planning. You'll need a full complement of fuel for the trip, as well as additional gas for unforeseen weather issues that may arise at SFO. The full fuel load might affect how much cargo you can take and how long the runway needs to be for your takeoff in Atlanta.

The weather will need to be scrupulously studied all along the route of flight. You will be traversing the entire continental United States, and the conditions may vary considerably. Passenger comfort becomes an important factor on a five-hour flight, so you'll need to ensure that the plane is catered with food and drinks, the lavatories are working, and whether to expect turbulence along the route.

Finally, you'll want to have a clear plan of action if an emergency arises. If a diversion to another airport is required, you'll need to get to an aerodrome that has runways long enough to handle your jet. They will also need to have facilities to accommodate your passengers, if required, and it would be nice if the airport was also a company destination with ground personnel familiar with your operations, including reliable mechanics who know your jet.

Similarly, in your business, entrepreneurial ventures, or personal aspirations, the planning process will be dictated by the ambitiousness of your vision. The bigger the goals, the more thoughtful and comprehensive the mission-planning process will need to be.

AIMING HIGH

I had embraced the vision of flying jets, and my mission now was to become an Air Force pilot. As I sat in my high school library, I realized that I had serious work ahead if I was going to figure out how to make my vision a reality. Even though early in life I assumed I would become a schoolteacher like other members of my family, I never gave much thought to the *process* I would need to follow to actually become one. Because I had numerous role models and mentors with a plethora of teaching information and experience, process was never front of mind.

But a military career presented a whole new ball game. My dad had been drafted into the Korean War as a corporal in the field artillery branch but separated as soon as his two-year obligation was up; I didn't think he was going to be much help with my lofty new aviation ambition. As I pondered my mission, I remembered having seen an Air Force recruiting station downtown near the post office, but I'd never given it a second thought. Now it seemed to be the logical place to go.

But sometimes what seems obvious isn't as simple as you might assume, and sometimes there are circumstances where your best intentions just don't work out. On my first visit, the office was closed—all locked up. On my second visit, the only recruiter in the office was an Army recruiter. Apparently, the different services shared the space, and not one to let an opportunity pass, the Army recruiter wasted no time in extolling the virtues of combat infantry. I knew from the nightly news that Vietnam was a hotbed of activity, and I was not excited about crawling around in the Southeast Asian jungles. I politely listened to his pitch but reiterated that I wanted to fly jets. I also stressed that I planned to go to college, so enlisting in the Army after high school wasn't an option. After almost having to fight my way out of the place, I gave my strategy another thought and headed back to the school library, where my research skills were improving markedly.

With the advent of the internet and Google, I expect that many younger folks today aren't as familiar with the complexity of doing research in a library under the old Dewey decimal system. The system used individual cardboard cards in endless wooden drawers (called catalogs). Each card had a three-digit Arabic numeral for main classes of books, with fractional decimals allowing for further expansion into more specific detail. Doing research this way was often a tedious and time-consuming process, but it was better than another visit to the recruiting station. With my luck, I was sure to get the Navy guy next.

I was beginning to zero in on the information I needed. I found general information on the Air Force as a service and then more specific info on the Air Force as a career. I learned the difference between the commissioned officer corps and the noncommissioned enlisted ranks. While certainly an oversimplification, the basic difference is akin to management and labor, with the officer corps being the management side of the house. It seemed a college degree was usually required to become a commissioned Air Force officer, and there were three ways to get one, two of which I felt were realistic to pursue:

> I could go to a college that had an Air Force ROTC (Reserve Officers' Training Corps) program. Within ROTC, there were two options: go to college and simply join the program, or apply for an ROTC scholarship and have the Air Force pay for part or all of my college education. With the latter option, I would be expected to stay in the Air Force for several years after graduation to pay the Air Force back for financing my education.

> I could go to the college of my choice on my own dime and after graduation go to Air Force Officer Training School (OTS) for ninety days. Upon satisfactory completion of the program, I would become a commissioned Air Force officer.

The third option involved going to the US Air Force Academy. I had heard of the Army's academy at West Point, New York, and the Navy's academy at Annapolis, Maryland, but I didn't even know there was an Air Force Academy. The information I read stated that the Air Force Academy in Colorado, the nation's newest service academy, was extremely competitive, both academically and physically, and was reserved for the select few.

I thought I could possibly compete academically and physically, but I wanted to know why the Academy was reserved for a select few. As I dug further, I discovered that the Academy was not for me: To compete for a small number of spots, you had to be nominated by your member of Congress, a US senator, or the vice president of the United States.

My congressman was a strict segregationist who had voted against every civil rights bill on the floor of Congress. My senior senator was Strom Thurmond, who was infamous for his racist views and for being the presidential nominee of the Dixiecrats, a segregationist third party in the 1948 presidential elections. And finally, my family was not politically connected in any way, so a vice presidential nomination was not even a plausible consideration. Given these realities, I dismissed the Air Force Academy as out of the realm of possibility. A regular college would be my bailiwick.

"It was good enough for me and your mom. It will be good enough for you."

I clearly remember the first time I discussed college with my dad. He was reading the newspaper in his favorite chair, and he didn't even put the paper down. His answer was short and to the point: "South Carolina State College." (SC State University today.) SC State is in my hometown of Orangeburg and is an HBCU, the acronym for Historically Black Colleges and Universities. It is also the alma mater of both my parents. My dad's reasoning was as succinct as his answer: "It was good enough for me and your mom. It will be good enough for you."

"State," as it was affectionately called, was an integral part of my life growing up. I was present at and vaguely remember both of my parents' graduations; my father and two of my uncles worked there for a time, so I had been on campus numerous times to visit them; and I had been involved in several kids' programs over the years, including dance, swimming, and basketball. But I had decided that I didn't want to go to college in my hometown. I wanted to see the world and get out from under the immediate influence (or supervision) of my parents. I therefore "informed" my dad that I didn't plan on going to State, though I had no idea of where I wanted to go at the time.

Still holding the newspaper, he did lower it to look at me. I can remember his exact words: "Your mom and I are paying for State. If you want to go somewhere else, you had better start working on a full scholarship." At least I clearly understood the financial parameters and the rules of the game.

With my newfound interest in flying (even though I had never flown on an airplane in my life) and the knowledge that I would need to finance my education if I didn't go to State, my mission planning began to take on more focus. I researched colleges that had ROTC programs—both Air Force and Navy—as a backup. I wasn't thrilled about being on a ship for six months at a time, but my Boy Scout training kicked in, and I figured it best to "Be Prepared" with other options.

The Army also had a substantial aviation branch but flew mostly helicopters and didn't require its pilots to be commissioned officers. With Vietnam having evolved into a full-fledged war, I figured I would eventually have to serve, but I didn't want it to be with the snakes, crocodiles, and other assorted and unappealing animals of Southeast Asia. I quickly eliminated the Army as one of my options.

So far, it seemed my wanting to "see the world" wasn't taking me very far from home. I discovered that the Military College of South Carolina (in Charleston, about sixty-five miles down Interstate 26 southeast of Orangeburg), better known as the

Citadel, had an Air Force ROTC program. I wrote to the admissions department and requested a catalog. I also found out that the University of South Carolina (USC, in Columbia, about forty-five miles up Interstate 26 northwest of Orangeburg) had a Naval ROTC program. With a catalog ordered from USC, I was beginning to feel pretty good about my current progress.

PAUSE, REGROUP, AND ORGANIZE

With research done and some initial action taken, I realized I needed to pause, regroup, and organize the information I had. I needed to develop some clear, simple steps to achieve the mission and a strategy to accomplish each of those steps. Planning the mission with a focus on excellence would be critically important to the ultimate outcome. I came up with a simple, four-step mission-planning process.

1. Find a college with an Air Force ROTC program to get a commission as an Air Force officer or one with a Navy ROTC program as a backup.

2. Identify how to get an ROTC or other university scholarship or some other funding.

3. Investigate more fully the Air Force OTS program.

4. Be clear on the process of how to get to flight training after college graduation and Air Force or Navy commission.

I got accepted to USC but was turned down for a Naval ROTC scholarship that would have paid for most of my education. I was still in the running for several other scholarships, but none that would cover all costs, so my interest in USC declined, given the monetary parameters set by my dad.

The Citadel was proving to be a much more promising option. Unfortunately, I had missed the deadline for the Air Force ROTC scholarship, but the school offered me a four-year scholarship that covered about 85 percent of the annual costs. I thought I could negotiate with my dad to cover the balance, since he and Mom had agreed to pay for South Carolina State. If I applied on time for the ROTC scholarship my sophomore year, between the two scholarships, I could cover all my costs. Things were looking up, and after a weekend campus visit in Charleston, I started getting used to the idea of becoming a Citadel cadet.

But my horizons changed dramatically when I received an unexpected letter from the National Merit Scholarship Corporation (NMSC). Apparently, I had done well on the standardized test they administered. They weren't going to give me a scholarship but congratulated me on my academic performance in relation to other high school students across the nation. I was happy to receive the letter, but because I wasn't getting any money, I didn't give it much more thought.

Then I started getting letters of congratulations on my NMSC honors along with admission catalogs from colleges all across the country. Many encouraged me to apply for admission, scholarships, and financial aid. I also received congratulation letters and catalogs from all five of the nation's service academies—the three military service academies that I had heard of and two others that I didn't know existed: the US Coast Guard Academy in New London, Connecticut, and the US Merchant Marine Academy in Kings Point, New York. This new information on the academies opened my eyes to possibilities I hadn't considered before. The Coast Guard had a significant flying operation, and the Coast Guard Academy did not require a congressional nomination to compete for an appointment like its four sister academies did. It was the only academy where entrance was strictly by nationwide competition. My interest in the Coast Guard Academy was immediate and significant.

The other significant information the service academy catalogs provided was detailed directions on how to apply for admission. There were instructions on how to write your senator and congressperson with sample letters and official addresses, lists of documents I would need to complete the application process, and how or where to obtain the required information. It was a complete, step-by-step process of how to get into an academy.

"Information and education can be potent forces that can take you to unimaginable and unbelievable places."

Those catalogs demystified the process for me, and as I read through the required steps, I reached the conclusion that applying to the academies was something I could pursue. Notwithstanding their civil rights records, I wrote both of my senators and my congressman, requesting nominations to the Air Force Academy. I also began the process of admissions with the Coast Guard Academy. I was now in the academy hunt—something that just weeks before I could not even have imagined. The takeaway for me was powerful. Information and education can be potent forces that can take you to unimaginable and unbelievable places.

In short order, I received letters from both of my US senators, who wrote that they were unable to provide me with a nomination. To my surprise, however, my congressman was giving me a sixth alternate nomination for the one spot he had been allocated to the Air Force Academy that year. I was underwhelmed with being so far down the list, but shortly thereafter I was contacted by the Air Force Academy to begin the admissions process. I learned that a member of Congress could nominate up to ten people for admission to the Academy for their one allocated slot—from the principal nominee to the ninth alternate. Because the Academy wouldn't know ahead of time which nominee would subsequently meet their qualifications, all of us were required to go through the same admissions process.

I soon received correspondence from the Coast Guard Academy: I had been accepted to apply. I was beyond excited knowing that if I was accepted, all my financial issues would be solved, and I would be in a position to pursue my vision to fly. With no congressional nomination needed, the Coast Guard Academy became my primary focus.

Charleston became the center of my universe. The nearest Air Force base and the nearest Coast Guard station were both in Charleston, and several components of the admissions processes required visits to those installations. I also kept in regular contact with officials at the Citadel and made it a point to stop by whenever I was in Charleston.

I was feeling pretty good about my mission execution. Though I had only obtained one firm financial commitment, I believed the Citadel was a great option, with the scholarship they offered and the opportunity to participate in Air Force ROTC. Being a sixth alternate nominee made the Air Force Academy a long shot. I felt like I was just going through the motions. But I was cautiously optimistic that the Coast Guard Academy might come through.

MISSION ACCOMPLISHED

One evening as I was grabbing a bite to eat, the phone in the kitchen rang. The caller said he was from the Coast Guard Academy, and I assumed he was calling to ask for additional information or to give me instructions for another Charleston visit. It was neither. Tad Schroeder, the head football coach at the Coast Guard Academy, wanted to know if I could fly up to New London to visit the Academy and talk about playing football for the Bears.

I was caught totally off guard. While I had enjoyed some success on the high school football field, I had decided not to play football in college; I wanted to concentrate on my studies and prepare myself for that ensuing aviation career. But the thought of playing college football got my competitive juices flowing. The thought of flying on an airplane to visit the Coast Guard Academy put me over the moon! The actual trip and visit were even better than I imagined. My very first flight ever amazed me. Lifting away from the earth was an incredible and thrilling feeling that I immediately loved. Imagining that this might actually be my job one day was almost unfathomable.

Coach Schroeder met me at the airport with a big welcoming smile. It was apparent that he was a class guy with a big heart and a professional attitude. We drove to the Academy, and the picturesque setting blew me away. Situated on a hill overlooking the Thames River, the campus venue could have been from a Norman Rockwell painting. He introduced me to two sharp but friendly cadets who would be my escorts over the following two days. The people I encountered were first class and the facilities better than anything I had ever encountered in my limited South Carolina experience.

When Coach Schroeder took me back to the airport on Sunday morning, I was sold—lock, stock, and barrel—on the US

Coast Guard Academy. And when he gave me an envelope containing a letter of appointment to the Academy, I was floored and overjoyed! Thankful beyond appreciation, I told Coach that I fully expected to be back for my summer admission and training in June. I did state the caveat that I couldn't give a firm commitment until I got home and discussed it with my parents. I then boarded that airplane for the second thrill of my life.

When I told my parents the great news about my fantastic Coast Guard Academy weekend, they were very happy and proud of me for setting a huge goal and accomplishing it, including taking care of the financial arrangements for my college education. There was much to share about the actual campus visit, but I was equally effusive in describing the thrill of my very first flights in a jet. My parents were likewise excited and anxious to hear every detail. In the process, my mother nonchalantly turned to me and said, "I almost forgot. You got another letter from the Air Force yesterday." I was thrilled about receiving my Coast Guard Academy appointment, but I opened the letter merely to see what additional information the Air Force might want from their sixth alternate nominee. To say that I was shocked is a gross understatement: The letter stated, "Congratulations! You have received an appointment to the United States Air Force Academy."

While I had been diligently going through the Air Force Academy process, I never expected to actually be in the running for an appointment, because I was so far down the nomination list. Receiving an appointment to the Air Force Academy should have been the highlight of my young life. Instead, it served to complicate it immensely.

With two appointments, I had just three days to make a decision about where to go. And despite being in an enviable position,

I was really stressed out. I now had an emotional connection with the Coast Guard Academy. They had invited me to the campus, and they had paid for the entire trip. They had enabled me to take my first airplane flight, which had been a life-changing experience. I knew good people there now, and they had treated me extremely well. I felt a deep sense of obligation for the total experience they had given me.

I didn't know anyone at the Air Force Academy and never visited the site, but there were many valid reasons to go Air Force. Only a small number of Coast Guard Academy graduates were selected to fly; the majority went to ships. So, it might be possible for me to fly, but becoming a pilot out of the Coast Guard Academy was the exception to the rule. At the Air Force Academy, I was guaranteed to fly if I was physically and pilot qualified. Also, I had loved my first flights over the weekend and could see myself doing that as my day-to-day job.

I went back and looked at the four-step mission-planning process I initially constructed. It helped me to refocus on my mission: to become an *Air Force* pilot. Ironically, the thrill of the flights I had taken to the Coast Guard Academy coupled with staying on goal helped me put emotion aside. I chose the Air Force Academy because I was guaranteed to fly. The first and foundational stage of my vision was complete: Mission accomplished!

THE TAKEAWAY

I have replicated the experience of getting into the Air Force Academy and the process I used to graduate and become a jet pilot many times in my personal and professional life. Creating a vision and planning a mission later got me into law school and, more important, out of it, to become an attorney. I used the same process to start and grow my first entrepreneurial enterprise into a successful business. Clearly defining *where I wanted to go and planning what I needed to do* to get there has proven to be a commonsense, repeatable, and effective method for the significant accomplishments I have been blessed with and enjoyed in life.

While this process can be universally applied in life, I believe it is absolutely critical if you also want to build a prosperous business or plot a successful professional career. Granted, sometimes things just happen. You may be in the right place at the right time, and fame and fortune just fall into your lap. (But I can't think of anyone in my immediate circle who has won the Mega Millions or Powerball.) Most of us have to have a plan.

Business owners, executives, and other "captains" who lead people need strong mission-planning efforts. Their flight crews need a clear understanding of the planned route so they can participate in reaching the destination and feel they are valued members of the team.

The mission in your business has the greatest effect when it becomes a *cause*. A mission becomes a cause when the vision is integrity based and service oriented, and when the team trusts its leadership and has a clear understanding of the route to be flown. People will work for money, but they will sacrifice for a cause.

During my early years at Delta, the company had a strong reputation for service, an enviable record of profitability, and was well known for taking care of its employees. The airline industry went through a tough time in the early 1980s due to deregulation, a weak economy, and increasing fuel prices. As a result, Delta suffered its first loss in over thirty-five years. But the company elected not to lay off any employees—the only major airline not to do so. To show our appreciation, we gave back a portion of our salaries to raise over $30 million ($200 million today) and bought the company a brand-new Boeing 767 jet christened *The Spirit of Delta*.

People will sacrifice for a *cause*.

It's also crucial for the captain to execute the mission with the passengers in mind. The customers have to continually be the focus of the mission in business. All too often, businesses focus on *company procedures* and not the customer. Even at Delta, a company with a sterling reputation for customer service, the focus was sometimes on procedure and not the customer.

For example, I recall a flight that had just arrived in Atlanta and the cabin crew had said good-bye to all the passengers. As the copilot and I were about to depart the airplane, I noticed an elderly woman sitting in the bulkhead aisle seat in first class. I asked her if she was OK. She told us she was waiting for a wheelchair. She also told us that she was worried she might miss her next flight because she had a very close connection. We told her we would check on the wheelchair status with the gate agent as we left.

With no wheelchair in sight, I asked the gate agent if she was aware of the passenger still on the airplane. She said she was and that she had called for a wheelchair rep. We explained that she had a close connection and asked if the agent had an ETA (estimated time of arrival) for the wheelchair. She did not. She had called for the wheelchair so, in her mind, the *company procedure* had been complied with. Yet the little old lady was sitting on the airplane and in danger of missing her connecting flight. Sometimes just complying with *procedure* is not enough. When necessary, you need to go above and beyond to get the job done. The mission was to get the elderly lady to her next flight.

The copilot grabbed an empty wheelchair from the next gate,

and we loaded the lady off the airplane. En route to her new gate, we ran into a rep with a motor cart who took her the rest of the way. Mission accomplished as she made her flight!

THE ASSOCIATION OF GRADUATES

Part of my vision as president and CEO of the Association of Graduates (AOG) at the Air Force Academy was to increase the connection our graduates had to the Academy and fellow grads. Anecdotal evidence suggested that the West Point and Naval Academy grads were more supportive of their institutions and closer with each other. As we studied the situation, the problem became fairly obvious: The Air Force Academy graduate community lacked a vibrant grassroots infrastructure to support its grads and keep them connected to the Academy.

Our study revealed that West Point had around 120 graduate alumni chapters and the Naval Academy had over 100. They both had a significant and strong grassroots infrastructure that gave their graduates a vehicle through which to connect on the local level and stay engaged with their academies. At the Academy, we had thirty-one graduate chapters, a total that had been static for a number of years. The mission to achieve the vision of connecting our graduates was to build a strong and vibrant chapter network with all deliberate speed. The Connection Project was born.

We determined how many graduates were required to establish a chapter and where our graduates were geographically clustered around the world. We then created a chapter handbook, which provided a turnkey process for those graduates interested in establishing a chapter. Our graduates

continued

are a fairly independent group, so it was important that the Connection Project not be perceived as a top-down effort from the national AOG. As such, the elements of the chapter handbook were recommended but not required.

To incentivize the chapters to follow the handbook, we established a Distinguished Chapter program that rewarded chapters that complied with our recommendations, with both recognition and financial enticements. A budget was established to properly resource the effort, and two out-standing young female academy grads, one Air Force and the other from West Point, were hired to implement the pro-gram. They traveled extensively around the country to assist with the chapter start-up efforts. Finally, the AOG sponsored a new annual Chapter Presidents Conference in the fall at the Academy in conjunction with a home football game.

The results greatly exceeded our expectations! We reason-ably assumed that we could more than double the number of chapters and set a reach goal of seventy. We also expected that approximately 10 percent of the chapters would qualify as Distinguished Chapters. Over a five-year period, we grew the number of alumni chapters to eighty-five. Twenty-one of our chapters attained the Distinguished Chapter recognition, or approximately 23 percent of the total number.

Mission accomplished and vision achieved!

Clearly defining and executing the mission is one of the most important criteria for attaining business, organizational, or personal success.

FOCUS ON EXCELLENCE:
THE SOAR + T GOALS

"By recording your dreams and goals on paper, you set in motion the process of becoming the person you most want to be. Put your future in good hands—your own."

–MARK VICTOR HANSEN,
American author
and motivational speaker

MOST PEOPLE HAVE meaningful things they would like to accomplish in life, but in reality, the majority never achieve their goals. According to an article in *Inc.* magazine, research conducted by the University of Scranton showed that a staggering 92 percent of people who set significant New Year's goals failed to achieve them.[11] If you were to ask why, you would get a host of reasons: not enough time, didn't know how, a lack of true motivation, and sometimes just plain fear. But if you interviewed that smaller group of people who have achieved excellence in their pursuits, you would discover among them some striking similarities. You would find that most had a laser-like focus on achieving their ambitions and a tried-and-true method of setting and accomplishing their goals.

The dictionary has several definitions for *focus*. One definition from physics defines focus as a point at which rays of light, heat, or other radiation meet after being refracted or reflected. Many of us can remember the classic example of this from childhood, when we took a magnifying glass and used it to focus the sun's rays on a piece of paper. If we did it correctly and held it long enough, the paper would burst into flames, creating an exciting event for all the kids watching the show.

Another definition of focus, of course, is to direct one's attention or efforts—which was what my parents or teachers would require when I wanted to play rather than do my homework after school. They wanted me to concentrate first on the things that were important and to put the noncritical or nontimely stuff aside. *This* definition has definitely become *my* definition for focus and *my* approach for getting the essential things accomplished in life.

The ability to focus on the key factors that will help you achieve excellence is essential. Not only does it channel your time and energy into doing the things that are most important

11   Vince Martinez, "How to Set Meaningful Personal and Business Results for 2019," *Inc.*, December 26, 2018, https://www.inc.com/partners-in-leadership/why-new-years-resolutions-fail-and-what-it-takes-to-succeed-all-year.html.

in accomplishing your goals, but focus also brings you assistance from people and other sources that you may not have recognized, were you not specifically focused on your objectives. One of the clear benefits of focus comes from the brain's ability to see things that would not have been readily apparent to you before you made focus a priority.

Let me give a quick, everyday example. Have you ever bought a new car? Even a used car counts because it was new for you. Well, as you drove around enjoying your new ride, what did you begin to notice? I bet you began to see the same model of your car more often than you had noticed before. In fact, you probably observed that many were also the same color. You undoubtedly thought in amazement, "I have a silver Toyota Corolla and it seems like everyone has a silver Toyota Corolla." Well, the reality is that those silver Toyotas were out there all the time, but until you got yours, there was no interest or reason for you to notice them. Yet they became readily recognizable to you once you were focused on them.

Similarly, when you are clearly focused on your pursuits, you'll begin to meet people, recognize resources, and encounter opportunities that are right on point with achieving your goals.

I have another point about being focused: It generally results in less stress and greater productivity all around. In short, by reducing stress, you will get more accomplished and be able to enjoy the process at the same time.

THREE WAYS TO FOCUS EFFECTIVELY

The process of focusing effectively on any effort consists of three parts.

1. First, you have to develop attention and concentration.

2. Second, you have to undertake an education process to learn as much as you can about the journey you are about to take.

3. Finally, you have to put goal setting center stage so you can zero in on the specifics needed to achieve a major outcome.

In today's world, focusing effectively is a major challenge because of the numerous distractions that grab our attention every day. Some of these are just the normal and obligatory actions that come with living, like spending time with loved ones, doing our daily tasks, and taking time to enjoy and recharge. Yet technology has brought a level of disruption few could have imagined even twenty years ago.

The internet and the smartphone are major impediments to maintaining focus and attention. The temptation to binge-watch on Netflix or Amazon has become an enticing and addictive diversion. It's hard for many people to get through a normal conversation without receiving a text or a notification from one of a million different apps—yet most folks won't disconnect from their phones for even a few moments. The result is that another day goes by and we haven't accomplished what we wanted to because our online time consumed the day. We're left wondering where the time went, but it doesn't take too much thought to figure it out.

PRIORITIZATION AND PERFORMANCE

To strive for and achieve excellence, we must focus our attention on the tasks that are of the greatest value to us and purposely and methodically put the distractions aside. Give yourself the time, space, and some boundaries inside of which you can concentrate on getting the important things done without allowing any interruptions from technology, colleagues, or even family and friends. Like most things in life, the more you practice this behavior, the better at it you will become. And repetition is the key to making prioritization and performance your default habits.

Once you master the attention challenge, you can proceed to the education process and set about acquiring as much knowledge and information as possible on what it will take to accomplish your mission. With the internet or Amazon Prime, information can be either at your fingertips or in your hands within a day or two. This is clearly one of the upsides to technology and can help immensely in your efforts to educate yourself.

But even though the technology of getting information has advanced immeasurably, it still takes effort on your part. You have to have the will to amass and consume the material you acquire. You have to read, study, listen to podcasts, or get your information in whatever way suits you best. You should also seek out other people who can help you—people who may be doing the exact thing that you want to do. Mentorship is always a good option for education, and the great thing about mentoring is that it can develop into so much more.

Some years ago, I was elected to the board of directors of a nonprofit organization. The chairman, a major Boston businessman, wanted to get the new directors involved quickly in board duties, and because of my willingness to take on these new responsibilities, we became friendly outside the organization. As a result, I was able to pick his brain on several business projects I was involved in or considering at the time. He was more than willing to provide valuable insight, and the information I received from him substantially improved the results of my business dealings.

THE BIGGEST GOAL

With the attention and knowledge phases completed, you can take the third step in the process of achieving excellence: goal setting. I have a story about a specific event to illustrate what I mean.

When the event occurred, I was going through Basic Cadet Training in the summer of 1969—my first at the Academy. Fifty years later, it's still satisfying for me to reflect upon one of the greatest examples of focus and goal setting in modern times, and which still remains arguably the most challenging and exciting scientific feat to date: man's landing on the moon.

KENNEDY'S MISSION

On May 25, 1961, President John F. Kennedy announced before a special joint session of Congress the dramatic and ambitious goal of sending an American to the moon with a safe return to Earth before the end of the decade. This was a goal that many thought both impossible and unattainable. Yet President Kennedy put the country's reputation on the line by looking to the future and setting a BHAG (Big Hairy Audacious Goal).

The motivation to go to the moon was both strategically

and politically driven, since at the time, the United States was involved in what was known as the Cold War with the Soviet Union. One important aspect of that war was the space race, in which the United States was trailing badly. The Soviets had been the first to put a satellite, Sputnik, into space in 1957, and the first to put a man into space—cosmonaut Yuri Gagarin, who orbited Earth on April 12, 1961.

Soon after, on May 5, 1961, the United States put astronaut Alan Shepard up, and his suborbital flight would make him the first American in space. It would take another nine months before astronaut John Glenn would become the first American to orbit Earth. While we were making progress, it was clear that the Soviet Union was still winning the space race.

President Kennedy went to NASA, the Department of Defense, and industry experts after Gagarin's flight to determine how we could get ahead of the Soviets. The consensus response was that with a tremendous effort and lots of money, we could conceivably get to the moon before the Soviet Union. After weeks of additional conversation, consideration, and contemplation, he made that now famous speech setting America after its most ambitious goal.[12]

I believe that this nation should commit itself to achieving the goal, before this decade is out, of landing a man on the moon and returning him safely to the earth. No single space project . . . will be more exciting, or more impressive to mankind, or more important . . . and none will be so difficult or expensive to accomplish.

—President John F. Kennedy, May 1961

continued

12 As a historical note, prior to the president's speech, the longest an American had been in space was fifteen minutes.

The pursuit of excellence was critically important as NASA began to focus on accomplishing this ambitious yet particularly dangerous national goal, and the space agency became singularly focused on achieving it. With all other distractions removed, the education phase began. Many missions were developed in order to explore the moon in great detail. NASA scientists wanted to understand the composition of its surface, determine what kind of weight it could support for a potential landing, and locate an appropriate landing site for a manned space effort. The Ranger, Surveyor, and Lunar Orbiter spacecraft probed the moon from every view imaginable to prepare for the arrival of manned flight.

At the same time, seven US astronauts, known as the Original Seven (Scott Carpenter, Gordon Cooper, John Glenn, Gus Grissom, Wally Schirra, Alan Shepard, and Deke Slayton), were going through rigorous training and beginning to fly a series of manned space flights to prepare for the eventual landing. Spearheaded by the Mercury program with Shepard and Glenn, the astronauts would graduate to more sophisticated spaceships in the Gemini program as their education progressed.

This education phase of the lunar program was comprehensive and wide ranging. In addition to studying the moon and developing larger and more powerful spacecraft, the effects on the astronauts themselves had to be taken into consideration. Not only was safety and basic survival of paramount concern, but food, hygiene, health, and clothing were also challenges that had to be overcome. Focus required education, and NASA paid attention to every imaginable aspect of the mission.

The Apollo program was the final leg of the lunar mission, culminating with Apollo 11, the flight that landed on the moon. With the crew of Neil Armstrong, Buzz Aldrin, and Michael Collins, the flight departed the Kennedy Space Center on July 16, 1969, just eight years after President Kennedy had set that original, ambitious goal. The spaceship entered lunar orbit on July 19.

On July 20, Armstrong and Aldrin climbed into the lunar module, called *Eagle*, and descended to the surface of the moon, leaving Collins in the orbiting command module. Upon touchdown, Armstrong famously stated, "Houston, Tranquility Base here. The *Eagle* has landed." Six and a half hours later, Armstrong came out of *Eagle*, climbed down its ladder, and stepped onto the moon, exclaiming his now famous celebration of the moment: "One small step for man, one giant leap for mankind."

When the moon landing occurred, during my first summer at the Air Force Academy, we were allowed by the upperclassmen to take a break in training to watch it on TV. It was an unforgettable moment. I felt a very strong connection to those astronauts who had all been military pilots—one Navy, the other two Air Force. The two Air Force pilots were also service academy grads. And I was at a service academy with the goal of becoming an Air Force pilot. It was exciting and surreal at the same time.

NASA and our country had achieved a spectacular accomplishment, which will forever be held as one of man's preeminent triumphs. In doing so, NASA had displayed a single-minded focus in achieving a monumental goal.

WRITE IT DOWN: THE POWER OF GOAL SETTING

The power of goal setting is unquestionable, as demonstrated by the moon-landing mission. It is equally powerful as a tool to achieve excellent outcomes in business and in life. Yet it is something that few people actually do because most aren't taught the importance of it.

Goals are the "lift beneath your wings." They are what take you to where you want to be. Goals help you to organize, prioritize, and achieve the things in life that others say they could never imagine having or doing.

Think of goals as the flight plan that gets you to your destination. When the captain takes off with a good flight plan, it will contain all of the critical information necessary for a successful flight. It will include the flight route, the fuel required, weather and winds along the route, and any likely turbulence along the way. With a good flight plan, updated during the flight, 99.9 percent of the time you'll arrive at your defined destination. Without a flight plan, you'll wander aimlessly until you run out of fuel and likely crash and burn.

> *"Think of goals as the flight plan*
> *that gets you to your destination."*

Academic research has shown that people who set goals are more likely to accomplish their desired outcomes than those who don't.[13] Professors Edwin A. Locke, from the Smith School of Business at the University of Maryland, and Gary P. Latham, from

---

13 A word of caution, though: Two so-called studies rampant on the internet are fictitious and were never conducted: "The Harvard Class of 1979" and "The Yale Class of 1953," which purport to show that the 3 percent of the class who wrote their goals down had amassed 97 percent of the classes' total wealth.

the Rotman School of Management at the University of Toronto (two preeminent academic researchers on goal setting), authored an article in the September 2002 issue of *American Psychologist* summarizing their thirty-five years of empirical research.

Some of the core findings include the following:

> ➢ Goals have an energizing function. High goals lead to greater effort than low goals.

> ➢ The highest or most difficult goals produce the highest levels of effort and performance.

> ➢ Specific, difficult goals consistently lead to higher performance than urging people to do their best.

> ➢ Making a public commitment to the goal enhances commitment, presumably because it makes one's actions a matter of integrity in one's own eyes and in the eyes of others.

> ➢ Tight deadlines lead to a more rapid work pace than loose deadlines.

Additionally, Dr. Gail Matthews, former chair of the psychology department at Dominican University of California, conducted a goal-setting study on how goal achievement in the workplace is influenced by writing goals, committing to goal-directed actions, and having accountability for those actions. Dr. Matthews found that participants who wrote down their goals and sent weekly updates to a friend had a much higher success rate than those who kept their goals to themselves.[14]

Dr. Matthews's research showed that when you focus, create,

---

14 Dr. Matthews presented her findings in May 2015 at the Ninth Annual International Conference of the Psychology Research Unit of Athens Institute for Education and Research (ATINER).

and then write your goals down, the process literally imprints the impression of actually achieving them in your mind. The written programing enhances your mental programming. When your goals are written, you can see them and refer back to them. And if you begin the morning by reviewing them, so they are consciously and unconsciously on your mind as you go through the day, you'll recognize countless opportunities that will help you in achieving them.

Pilots have detailed *written* checklists for every phase of a flight. Let me list them so you'll capture the full impact of that fact. There are the Before start, Engine start, After start, Taxi, Before takeoff, After takeoff, Cruise, Descent, Approach, Before landing, After landing, and Shutdown checklists. No matter how long you have been flying, you always go through the checklists. Why? Because the things we need to do that are critically important have to be done right, and they are too important to commit to memory. They have to be written down.

Your goals are critically important to getting what you want out of life. Your family, your career, your financial security, and your personal development are all key components of your existence. Write your goals down, because they need to be done right. They are too important to try to commit to memory.

SOAR + T

Once you understand the importance of written goals in attaining excellence in your quests, you'll also need to develop a goal-setting paradigm that works. All too often, goals are set with no clear process adopted to achieve them. Is it any wonder that most people fail to achieve their stated goals?

Making a to-do list is not the same as setting goals. We have to make a disciplined effort in the goal-setting process because there are distinct characteristics that define a good goal. Sometimes the goal itself is problematic. If it's too vague, it can set you up for failure. Sometimes progress on achieving the goal is difficult to measure. And frequently, we don't set a time frame within which we will accomplish the goal—which is the death knell to ever getting it done.

The SOAR + T goal-setting method is an excellent tool to help you set goals that are well defined, are motivational, and have a great possibility of actually being accomplished. In true military fashion, SOAR + T is an acronym, which stands for SPECIFIC, OBJECTIVE, ATTAINABLE, REALISTIC + TIME-BOUND. This will be the measuring standard as you set clear goals that will rocket you to your chosen destination.

SPECIFIC

You must clearly define what you want, and why it is important that you have it. You want a mental picture of what it looks like, feels like, and what you are willing to give up for it in terms of time, work, or money.

I have a good friend who for years has talked about having a vacation home in some exotic place. When I ask him where, he's never specific. He says maybe in the Caribbean so he can enjoy the beach—or maybe in Colorado. We both went to school in Colorado, and he has dreamed about having a place there so he can enjoy the mountains and the skiing. I've asked him how large a place he would need. He doesn't know—two bedrooms or maybe three. I've asked him how much he would spend. He doesn't know. I've asked him when he is going to move on his dream. "Maybe in a couple of years," he says. It's now forty years later, and he's still having the same conversation. Until he gets SPECIFIC, he'll never own that home.

OBJECTIVE

There should be objective criteria that you can measure on your progress toward achieving your goal. You, or I, or a disinterested third party should be able to track your progress on achieving the goal.

Being rich, for example, is not an objective goal. Your definition and mine of the amount of money it takes to be rich might be completely different, and for someone else, being rich might not involve finances at all. A goal to have a million dollars is objective. We can all track your progress toward achieving that goal.

ATTAINABLE

There are some things we just can't do, period. There may be practical, legal, or financial considerations that make attaining a goal impossible. It doesn't move your life forward to focus on something that can't be done. If you are sixty-four years old with two hundred hours of flying time, you aren't going to be hired by Delta as a commercial airline pilot, because the minimum number of hours required is fifteen hundred and mandatory retirement is sixty-five. You've missed that opportunity. That goal is clearly unattainable.

REALISTIC

This is not to say that you should not set ambitious goals. I'm a big fan of "shooting for the stars" in life, and we often underestimate what our true potential is. That said, we do need to have some realistic expectation that it will be possible for us to achieve the goal, even if it is a stretch goal.

You'll recall from my story at the end of Chapter 10 about growing the AOG membership that we had thirty-one alumni chapters across the country, and we figured we could realistically double the number we had. We set a stretch goal of seventy, which was about 13 percent higher than what we expected we could do. In the end, we actually established eighty-five chapters, which was way beyond our expectation. Notwithstanding that great success, it would have been unrealistic to establish a goal of 150 chapters at the outset, as there just weren't enough alumni to populate that level of growth.

+ TIME-BOUND

Establish a realistic deadline by which to have your goal accomplished. It is human nature to procrastinate. That deadline will put pressure on you to see things through. Do you remember from your school days when you had a project or a paper due? That deadline forced you to get it done on time. Keep the pressure on yourself and you'll feel a marked sense of accomplishment when you get the job done.

While to-do lists are not goals, they can play an important part in achieving your goals. They are the way to break your goals down into the component parts of what needs to be done. Make your list with the most important things you need to do each day. You may not be able to do everything, but you can always do the important things. Transfer those things that didn't get accomplished to the list for the next day and then reprioritize. Always designate the top three things that you will absolutely achieve that day and then move on down the list. You'll get a real sense of accomplishment when you can check something off and even more of one when you achieve your goal.

Finally, as you go through the goal-setting process, be clear on what you want and why—on the deepest level possible. Sometimes we can set a goal that meets all of the criteria of the SOAR + T process but does not actually reflect what we really want. When I was thirty, I set a goal of having a two-seat Mercedes convertible with a phone in it. This was before both Mercedes and cell phones were prolific, and having a phone in a car was a big deal. When I achieved that goal, I realized that my real goal was to have financial security at an early age in life. The car and the phone were just manifestations of what should have been my primary goal.

Being focused and setting and accomplishing goals are the jet engines that provide the thrust for your Flight to Excellence. With the SOAR + T goal-setting process, you'll have the instruments that will power you to heights you may have thought unreachable.

=PART IV=

PERFORMANCE

"The most difficult thing is the decision to act. The rest is merely tenacity. The fears are paper tigers. You can do anything you decide to do. You can act to change and control your life and the procedure. The process is its own reward."

—AMELIA EARHART,
American aviation pioneer

YOU HAVE TO EXECUTE
TO FLY THE JET

"Do or do not. There is no try."

—YODA, Jedi master, *The Empire Strikes Back*

MOST OF US are familiar with one of the bedrock principles of action. The renowned physicist Sir Isaac Newton's third law states that for every action, there is an equal and opposite reaction. The reaction for your dedicated action will be the ultimate attainment of excellence in your pursuits, endeavors, and accomplishments.

———

Congratulations! You've now read about all the steps that are required to prepare for a successful Flight to Excellence.

We've discussed the importance of having the right fundamental principles in place as your foundation. You understand how critical it is to have a talented copilot and to gather a brilliant flight crew. You've come to appreciate the potential opportunities that may come your way when you engage the fascinating passengers on your flight. You know that a great flight plan must have the vision defined and mission planning complete. And surrounded by the right people, you and your flight crew can develop an effective and efficient flight plan to get you to your desired destination.

But now, as the captain, you'll need to take action to actually fly the plane. You'll have to push the throttles up to power the engines, steer the jet down the runway, pull back on the controls, and get that giant metal bird in the air. Once airborne, you'll be able to pilot that jet at amazing speeds to lofty altitudes and fly great distances to any destination around the world. Likewise, achieving great heights and traveling far in life also require proper preparation. But in life as in flying, taking action is the final and most important step. Action is the jet engine that propels you toward achieving your goals.

> *"Action is the jet engine that propels*
> *you toward achieving your goals."*

Some (if not most) people find it difficult to take action, because it's human nature to procrastinate. It's a challenge that we will all face at one time or another. Somehow, we can invariably find innumerable reasons to do just about any type of mundane activity rather than attending to the important things we really need to do in order to move ahead. Procrastination is the drag that keeps us from flying high in our lives.

WHY WE STALL OUT

Why, then, do we procrastinate? The science on the subject is informative, and different people procrastinate for different reasons. Let's look at some of the more common causes to see if any of them apply to you. Then I'll offer some suggestions that may help you recover from your particular stalled approach and get you back on course and flying toward your goals.

STALL #1: LACK OF MOTIVATION

Lack of motivation is the most common reason people give for their tendency to procrastinate. Even getting motivated to do things that are obviously of personal benefit, like hitting the gym, can be a challenge—much less attending to things like cleaning the house or mowing the lawn. And sometimes, we just don't feel like doing anything; dare I say, we just feel lazy?

THE LACK OF MOTIVATION STALL RECOVERY

The only antidote to a lack of motivation is to just get started on whatever the project is. Just that one small step that begins the task will often give you the motivation that was missing before. So, your challenge is not to develop the motivation *beforehand* to complete the job. It is to start the task, and the motivation usually will quickly follow.

STALL #2: FEELING OVERWHELMED

The size of the task at hand may seem overwhelming. Let's say you've got to produce a thirty-page report and just gathering the research is going to take a tremendous effort. Maybe it's the complexity of the job that might be the issue. Maybe it's going to require technical knowledge, and you are not a "techie." You don't know where to start. So you don't.

THE FEELING OVERWHELMED STALL RECOVERY

Sit down, take a deep breath, and put your thinking cap on. You'll want to figure out how you can take this large or complicated task and break it down into smaller, manageable parts. Sometimes this is called "chunking." It's a process that will allow you to focus on the more unwieldy parts of the larger project and give you both a process and the motivation to work it through. If technology or a particular skill set is the issue, you will want to focus on what you can accomplish and then plan to seek the appropriate help on the parts that may require additional expertise.

STALL #3: YOU'RE BORED

The task at hand is boring to you, and you can't build up the motivation to begin to tackle it. Lack of interest or avoiding a particular topic can often develop when you can't see the relevance of it to your longer-term goals.

THE YOU'RE BORED
STALL RECOVERY

Sad but true: Not everything we need to do in life lights our afterburners. Many of the things we may have to do on our flight to higher goals are just not that interesting or enjoyable. I love to read and am fascinated by reading about things that have actually happened. As a result, I majored in history at the Air Force Academy. I never liked math much, but the Academy is essentially an engineering school, and to get to my goal of sitting in the cockpit of a supersonic jet, I had to get through the science, math, and engineering courses. Sometimes we just need an attitude check. It's a matter of accepting that to get to that higher level of accomplishment you want to achieve, you have to get through some things that may not be that exciting.

STALL #4: PERCEIVED LACK OF SKILL

You may doubt your skill or whether you have the ability to get a particular task done. If we don't know how to attack a particular problem, it's quite understandable that we'll be inclined to procrastinate. How many times have you heard someone say, "I could never do that"? This kind of thinking can become a self-fulfilling prophecy.

THE PERCEIVED LACK OF SKILL STALL RECOVERY

No one was born knowing what we know today. We have studied, practiced, and learned all that we have come to know. It's the natural growth pattern in life that we have all experienced. The key to solving a problem is to understand what the problem is, and in this case, it is probably a knowledge or skills gap.

The first step is to confirm that the gap actually exists by trying to tackle the issue yourself. You may find that your preconceived notion was wrong. If you need help or instruction, get it from either colleagues or professionals in the field.

STALL #5: SHORT-TERM FOCUS

Some people find it easier to focus on activities that will bring a shorter-term, less consequential reward than to focus on a project that will bring much more value in the longer term. Neuroscience studies conclude that we are hardwired to prioritize shorter-term rewards over longer-term gains.[15] That's why it is easier to check our emails than to begin writing an article to put on LinkedIn.

---

15 Melissa Chu, "Why Your Brain Prioritizes Instant Gratification, *Inc.* magazine, July 30, 2017, https://www.inc.com/melissa-chu/why-your-brain-prioritizes-instant-gratification-o.html.

THE SHORT-TERM FOCUS STALL RECOVERY

This requires some talking. Start out by talking to yourself. Remind yourself why you are doing what you are doing and what the longer-term payoff is going to be. Talk to others who have been through a similar situation. Their insight, encouragement, and mentoring may help give you the motivation to get back on track.

I have a friend whose son was in his first year at West Point. He wanted to quit because things weren't going well. My friend asked if I would talk to him to provide my insight as a service academy graduate. During a forty-five-minute chat, I was able to help him put his current challenges into perspective while emphasizing the long-term benefits of being a West Point graduate. He went on to have a successful tenure as a cadet and is now serving as an officer in the US Army.

You can also develop new habit patterns that are focused on your longer-term journey. Begin by doing small things that you can build upon, and then increase your actions as you begin to improve. With consistency and patience, you'll transform both your mindset and your actions as you solidify your progress and enjoy your longer-term success.

STALL #6: YOU ARE A PERFECTIONIST

You are a nitpicker about every detail, and everything has to be just right before you can get started on any project. You have to have the perfect mindset, the perfect environment, and your material perfected before you can begin the work.

THE YOU ARE A PERFECTIONIST STALL RECOVERY

An old saying attributed to the great French philosopher Voltaire is often used in business today: "Don't let the perfect be the enemy of the good." The fact is perfection is often an impossible standard to achieve. So, if you are waiting for perfection, you'll run the high risk that nothing will ever get done. Conversely, there are a lot of things worth doing that can be done "good." You don't have to strive for the bodybuilder's shape to be motivated to go to the gym. Looking good and being in good health can be motivation enough to get to the health club a few times a week. Accept the "good," be productive, and keep flying forward.

STALL #7: FEAR HOLDS YOU BACK

I've seen a lot of clever acronyms for FEAR over the years, so naturally, I had to come up with one of my own: Failure of Excellence, Achievement, and Rewards. I'll admit that this is a bit of a stretch, but essentially, by **F**ailing to strive for **E**xcellence, you'll also fail to **A**chieve and miss out on the accompanying **R**ewards. The crippling power of FEAR can paralyze us and prevent us from taking the action necessary to achieve our goals. There are several reasons that we can become fearful, and they all can stop us dead in our tracks. Let's look at three different types of fear and how they cause us to procrastinate.

Fear of failure. Some folks are devastated when they don't achieve a goal or accomplish what they strive for. They can be obsessed with not getting things right or unrealistically fixated on messing things up. They view a failure as irreparable damage to their status, whatever they assume that to be. Sometimes these negative feelings can be so overpowering that the motivation to pursue the goal is completely overcome with the feeling that it's not even worth it to try.

THE FEAR OF FAILURE
STALL RECOVERY

This is a naive and unhealthy view of failure. Failure is an important part of the learning and growth process and is inherent in our development from the very beginning of our lives. We all failed at trying to walk the first time. We fell down, got up, and tried it again. We all kept trying until we finally took those first few steps, to the excitement of our parents. And we've been walking ever since. Anytime we are pushing ourselves to try something different or to learn something new, we are bound to make mistakes and have setbacks along the way. Our failures are the pavement on the road to greater achievement in life. You'll need to accept this as the natural order of things.

Fear of success. As odd as it may seem to some, there are many people who are actually afraid of succeeding, and this fear triggers their inability to accomplish certain tasks. The genesis of this fear comes from an irrational focus on what people perceive to be the negative aspects of being successful. For example, being successful may bring on greater obligations, require more of your time, or cause greater stress. There may also be a fear of greater expectations—you were good the first time, and this time we expect you to be great! And you may feel that you are just not ready for success. We have all read the stories of people who have achieved great fortune and fame but couldn't handle it and have crashed and burned.

THE FEAR OF SUCCESS STALL RECOVERY

The first step in solving any problem is to understand that you have one. Examine your feelings at a deeper level and see if any of the reasons discussed above apply to you. The next step is to understand why you feel the way you do. Set aside some time to give it serious thought. Take some notes to help out. The more you understand the "why," the better your chances of dealing with those feelings successfully. Finally, come up with a strategy to deal with the "why" that has been sabotaging your progress. Start by doing little things to get you on a positive path. That's how habits are developed or changed. The goal is to change your mindset about the way you have been viewing success and to realize that your perception of the things that accompany success are not, in fact, negative but are usually positive aspects that come with achieving your goals.

Fear of embarrassment. Being embarrassed is a common situation and one that we have all shared. We can find ourselves in it due to some very simple circumstances, like unintentionally saying something inappropriate in front of others or doing something that is publicly unacceptable. This fear of embarrassment can keep us from doing things we need to do, like failing to ask a question in a group for fear of what others might think.

The fear of embarrassment can become extreme for some people and stop them dead in their tracks, and they can become paralyzed by what other people might think. It can strangle your self-confidence, hold you back from taking calculated risks, and keep you from flying high to reach your full potential.

THE FEAR OF EMBARRASSMENT STALL RECOVERY

First and foremost, don't automatically assume that others care about what you are feeling embarrassed about. As a mentor of mine once told me, "Don't point out the stain on your tie. Most people will never notice it until you point it out."

Try not to care about what people think. You can't please everyone anyway, so focus on your own path. That is, stay true to your own principles. Own who you are and how you are. If you make an embarrassing blunder, take responsibility for it. Most people are very forgiving of a mistake, especially when you acknowledge it. Finally, find a way to use embarrassment to spur you to action. Use it as motivation to change and be better at the things you need to do.

HOW FEAR HELD ME BACK

It was the second semester of my junior year at Orangeburg High. A new girl had transferred to the school from out of town, and I was immediately smitten by her attractiveness and sweet personality. She was in several classes with me, and I spent a lot of class time just looking at her. This was during my shy phase of life, so while we did exchange some hellos, I wasn't confident enough to try to engage her in a real conversation.

There were several other guys who did talk to her, and I was jealous, though I had no reason to be. Besides, my jealousy wasn't enough motivation to spur me to action. One of the guys she chatted with was a senior and a star on the basketball team, and I noticed that he talked to her a lot. I naturally assumed that she liked him as well.

The junior/senior prom was soon coming up, and I really wanted her to go with me, but I was too shy and afraid to ask her. I suspected that she would be going with the basketball star, and, through the grapevine, I discovered that I was right. I asked another girl who thought I was cute and who I knew had a crush on me. Even though she wasn't my first choice, we had a pretty good time. But I spent a good part of the evening looking (clandestinely, of course) at my dream date and the basketball star, all the while wishing I were in his place.

A few days later, I was talking to a close friend of mine who asked me how I had enjoyed the prom. I told her that I had a good time, but I confided in her that it was the new girl I had really wanted to take. Her demeanor immediately changed, and she said, "Why didn't you ask her?" I told her that I knew she would be going with the basketball star, so it would have been a wasted effort. She called me a "dummy" and told me I had blown it. I was totally confused. She told me that she had talked to the new girl the day after the prom. My dream date told my friend that she liked me and had really wanted to go to the prom with me, but I had never asked her. She reluctantly went with the basketball star because he was the only one who asked, and she told my friend that she had a terrible time.

I was shocked, but even more so, I was greatly disappointed in myself. It hurt me deeply to know that I could have had exactly what I wanted if I had only had the courage to ask. I promised myself right then and there that I would never again allow FEAR to keep me from going after something that I really wanted.

The fact is that most of the things we are afraid of are imagined, like the monsters in the dark or the boogeyman we feared as kids. To a huge extent, fear is the result of our erroneous perceptions, like my assumptions about my dream date. One person can see a large dog and think it is the cutest thing in the world. Another person can see the same dog and be terrified to death. But it's the same dog. You can't allow your fear to let you miss out on some fantastic rewards on your journey to high achievement. Having the courage to go after the things you really want can bring you unexpected joys in life.

REWARDS OF TAKING ACTION

Woody Allen said, "Eighty percent of success is just showing up." To be honest, I'm not the biggest fan of Woody Allen, but I must admit that I like the quote. And over time, I have found it to be generally true. Just by taking action and showing up, I have acquired several significant opportunities during my entrepreneurial career.

When I was invited to Subway World Headquarters for a tour, I wasn't that enthused and really didn't want to go. It was a two-and-a-half-hour drive from Boston to Milford, Connecticut, and between the driving and the tour, it was going to be an all-day affair. It was a busy time for me, and I had more important things to do. Besides, I had already made the contact at Pizza Hut, which I found much more attractive, and owning a sub shop did not ring my bell. And at the time, I had never heard of Subway. But I decided to take the trip and "show up," in great part out of a sense of obligation to my new friend who had given me the contact. By taking action, I met the founder of Subway on my tour and the rest, as they say, is history.

I believe the true meaning of the 80 percent quote is that you have to put some effort into whatever it is you want to achieve. I hear a lot of people talk about the big ideas they have or what they plan to do, but years later, they've taken no action. It's the same old tune: Time keeps moving on, and no progress has been made. "Showing up" means you are doing more than just *talking* about your ideas and dreams or complaining about the things you don't like. It means that you are taking some concrete action to get yourself to where you truly want to be.

Sometimes progress takes time—weeks, months, and even years. But that's OK, as long as you are growing, advancing, and continuing to move in the right direction. I started law school at the ripe old age of twenty-six, four years after I had graduated from the Academy. But most of my classmates were just out of college, and I was one of the older students in my class. Law school for me was going to be a four-year program because I was in the evening division. I realized that it would be a long haul, but I figured, "Four years from now, I'm going to be thirty. I can be thirty with or without a law degree. All things considered, it's better to have the degree." So, I took action and started moving forward toward this brave new goal. And yes, law school was hard work, and at times, it was a toil. But it was smart work because it gave me options in my professional career and eventually opened doors for me that were unimaginable when I was going through the grind.

SUPREME COURT JUSTICE LEWIS POWELL

Taking action sometimes requires hard work, but the key to moving forward is to make sure the work you are doing is smart work and designed to get you closer to your larger goal.

I have admired former Supreme Court Justice Lewis Powell since my days in law school. I think it was because we had some career aspects in common. He was a lawyer who also served operationally in what would become the US Air Force. I haven't always agreed with his opinions, but I found him to be a man of great character and a justice willing to compromise. Through his work ethic he demonstrated that he was also committed to taking action and performing with excellence throughout his entire career.

A son of Virginia, Powell attended Washington and Lee University, graduating magnum cum laude and Phi Beta Kappa. He returned to Washington and Lee to attend law school, graduating number one in his class. Powell went on to earn a master of laws degree from Harvard and is one of only two Supreme Court justices to have earned the LLM degree.

continued

A natural leader, Powell served as student body president while at Washington and Lee, as well as managing editor of the college newspaper and president of his fraternity. He went on to serve his community as chairman of the Richmond school board and later as chairman of the state board of education.

At the outbreak of World War II, Powell left his big law firm in Richmond to volunteer for service in the US Army Air Corps. He served in the North African and European theaters and rose to the rank of colonel. He received the Legion of Merit, the Bronze Star, and the French Croix de Guerre with bronze palm for his heroic service. He was discharged in October 1945 and returned to the practice of law at his former firm in Richmond.

Powell enjoyed an exceptional legal career, serving as president of the American Bar Association before being appointed to the Supreme Court by President Richard Nixon. A conservative by disposition, he would become the swing vote and voted with the liberal wing of the court on many major cases including *Roe v Wade.* He also struck compromise positions on both affirmative action and major death penalty cases. Doug Wilder, the first elected African American governor in the United States, asked Powell to swear him into office in 1990.

When asked once by a reporter how he had been able to enjoy such a stellar career, Powell stated, "I worked hard; some others didn't." Justice Powell is the epitome of a person driven to take action, and it accounted for his tremendous personal and professional success.

READING IS NOT ACTION

As I mentioned before, I love to read, and I have learned a lot from my readings about a plethora of different things. Yet my reading has also taught me that knowledge is often no substitution for action. In most cases, it's not what you know that is important. *It's what you do with what you know that gets rewarded.* You can read volumes of manuals on how to fly different types of airplanes, and I have had to do that many times in my long aviation career. Yet until you get in the cockpit and take action to maneuver the controls, you won't know what it is like to actually fly that plane.

And even with that extensive base of read knowledge and having taken the first step to get into the cockpit and fly the jet, you won't immediately get it right. You'll make mistakes and screw things up until you learn the proper methods and figure out the techniques that work for you.

As time progresses and you continue to put the effort in, your skill will develop, and you will become more accomplished. The more you practice, the higher your level of proficiency and excellence will become. What had been a struggle will become habit. *Habit* is defined by Dictionary.com as "an acquired behavior pattern regularly followed until it has become almost involuntary." Habit is what you strive for. Habit is the result of taking action and getting where you want to be. Habit is your ultimate goal.

A quote attributed to the great Greek philosopher Aristotle sums it up well:

> *"We are what we repeatedly do. . . . Excellence*
> *then, is not an act, but a habit."*

Here's another quote I once heard the renowned motivational speaker Les Brown use in a presentation. This great line has stuck with me over the years:

> *"You don't have to be great to get started, but*
> *you have got to get started to be great."*

Find that thing that motivates you to action; it might be anger, disgust, or desire. Acquire a sense of urgency and develop a bias toward doing it now. Getting started often requires you to get out of your comfort zone and to push your personal envelope, but that is what's required to learn, achieve, and grow.

DETERMINATION: FLYING THROUGH THE TURBULENCE

I'VE FLOWN MY passengers to some of the most beautiful places around the world, and the overwhelming majority of those flights were smooth and uneventful, which is exactly how pilots want them to be. But occasionally, we had significant challenges to overcome in order to successfully complete the flight. Sometimes mechanical problems arose. On other occasions, passenger issues needed to be addressed.

But more often, thunderstorms, turbulence, or other bad weather were the reasons for an uncomfortable ride along the route. Pilots don't want to let any obstacles stop a flight, whether they originate on the ground or in the air. And of course, there is the obvious: Once airborne, pilots don't have the option of pulling over and parking the jet on the side of the road. When the captain anticipates bad weather, he'll take on thousands of pounds of extra fuel. This gives him the option of traveling hundreds of miles off course to avoid dangerous storms or to divert to another airport if the arrival weather turns bad. The captain does whatever is necessary to provide the passengers with a safe flight to their final destination.

Just as pilots do, each of us faces challenges in our daily lives that have to be overcome. In most instances, if we are lucky, we are dealing with relatively minor issues that are more irritants than crises. Most of us deal with these minimal issues without too much effort and continue on our daily paths. But sometimes that's not the case. We may have to deal with larger or even potentially life-changing issues that test our soul and call upon our resilience to make it through. These instances require us to step up, shake it off, and do whatever is necessary to navigate through the turbulence of life. These times call for a mindset of determination. Only a mindset of determination will get you through the tough times and enable you to achieve your planned goals.

WHAT IS DETERMINATION?

Determination can have several meanings, but in the context of this conversation, let's focus on *the quality of being resolute, of having firmness of purpose*. And while that definition succinctly captures one of the definitions of being persistent, let me expand on that meaning based on my personal experiences with determination.

I define determination as having mental toughness and *stick-to-it-ness*. It's being able to go the extra mile when you would really rather not. It's being professional at what you do and doing it with excellence, even when you are not at your best or when you are having a bad day. The necessity of building a mindset of fortitude, grit, perseverance, and sheer determination cannot be overstated.

> *"Fortitude, grit, perseverance, and sheer determination cannot be overstated."*

The good news is that we all have the potential to show those characteristics, because determination is a skill that can be learned. On a basic level, and fortunately for most of us, it's a quality that we already possess—the ability to be stubborn at times. The classic example is the husband who is driving aimlessly and is obviously lost but steadfastly refuses his wife's suggestion to stop and ask for directions. The challenge is to channel that tendency to be stubborn into the positive trait of determination.

WHY DETERMINATION IS IMPORTANT

We are all enjoying the privilege of living life, but as I've said, life will be tough at times. OK. I get it. This is supposed to be a motivational book, and that statement doesn't sound very inspiring. But it is important to deal with realities and not focus on how we wish things could be. The fact is we are going to have failures, setbacks, and adversity as we pilot our Flight to Excellence, and you don't want those temporary obstacles to be an excuse for giving up on achieving your goals.

It doesn't matter who you are—you'll have to deal with hardship at times. You could be the wealthiest or most powerful person in the world, and you would still have your bad days. We need look no further than the examples of recent presidents to prove the point. Nixon: Watergate, resigned; Carter: the Iran hostage crisis; Reagan: victim of an assassination attempt; Bush 1: didn't get reelected; Clinton: was impeached; Bush 2: 9/11; Obama: the Great Recession; Trump: also impeached.

Even the richest man in the world, Jeff Bezos, has had his tough times. One of his recent challenges was going through a divorce with his longtime wife. According to news reports, the divorce settlement gave his now ex-wife $38 billion, making her the fourth-richest woman in the world.[16] So even being extremely wealthy or powerful doesn't insulate you from the trials and tribulations of life.

Accepting this reality allows you to lay the foundation for developing a determination mindset. You'll be able to keep the turbulence you encounter in perspective and stay focused and motivated as you work to achieve a particular goal. Being a determined pilot increases your odds of being successful in those endeavors and accomplishing the important things in life you want to achieve.

---

16 Rupert Neate, "Amazon's Jeff Bezos Pays Out $38bn in Divorce Settlement," *The Guardian*, June 30, 2019, https://www.theguardian.com/technology/2019/jun/30/amazon-jeff-bezos-ex-wife-mackenzie-handed-38bn-in-divorce-settlement.

Most of us are familiar with the saying "If it was easy, every-one would do it." You have even probably said it yourself. The actual quote is slightly different and comes from the 1992 movie *A League of Their Own*—about a women's professional baseball league during World War II. Coach Jimmy Dugan, played by Tom Hanks, is talking to one of his players, Dottie Hinson, who is played by Geena Davis. She has just quit their team right before they are to play in the World Series. She tells Coach, "It just got too hard." Coach Dugan's response: "It's supposed to be hard. If it wasn't hard, everyone would do it. The hard is what makes it great."

In truth, the path to your greatness does get hard at times and can have obstacles that test who you really are. But it is also true that you *can* get to that level of personal or even public great-ness. *Most* people can. The question is, do you have the willpower to take the flight and navigate through the turbulence when you begin to have that bumpy ride? When I think about this topic, I think of a quote attributed to Calvin Coolidge, our thirtieth US president, which I have long admired and found to be accurate time after time:

> Nothing in this world can take the place of persistence.
> Talent will not: nothing is more common than unsuc-cessful men with talent.
> Genius will not: unrewarded genius is almost a proverb.
> Education will not: the world is full of educated derelicts.
> Persistence and determination alone are omnipotent.

Mather Air Force Base in Sacramento was totally socked in, and the supervisor of flying (SOF) asked me to launch a flight as the weather ship to determine just how high the weather ceiling was. I grabbed my student to give him some real-life instrument time, and we headed off to the flight line to fire up the jet.

We were in the weather at 500 feet above the runway and stayed in it all the way up to 25,000 feet as we headed out over the Sierra Nevada mountains to practice instrument maneuvers in our work area. We had just gotten established in the area when we lost our attitude indicator—the primary and most important instrument that is used to fly in the weather. It has a small airplane displayed on a gyroscopic globe and tells pilots whether they are flying straight and level, climbing or descending, or turning left or right. It also gives precise information on a degree scale so that you know exactly how much the jet is climbing, descending, or turning. On a clear day, the attitude indicator is not as important because you can just look out of the cockpit and visually keep your orientation. But when your visual cues look like you are in the inside of a ping-pong ball, having the attitude indicator is how you fly the jet, and it is truly critical.

We told air traffic control that we had a serious problem and needed to switch frequencies to talk with our SOF. The SOF immediately understood the gravity of our situation, and we discussed the condition and began to prepare for the probability of ejecting from the jet. We gave our location as accurately as we could (the Air Force GPS system was not operational at that time), and the SOF prepared to send rescue helicopters our way.

While ejecting was certainly a strong option, I was determined not to eject in the weather over the rugged mountains below, and miles away from civilization. I told the SOF that I would try to fly the plane using a very difficult procedure called "needle, ball, and airspeed" before abandoning the jet. In that procedure, a pilot uses secondary flight instruments to determine the airplane's attitude. For example, if the airspeed is increasing, you know that the jet is descending, and if the airspeed is decreasing, you know that the jet is in a climb. But you won't know how much either way.

There is also another small instrument tucked down in the corner of the instrument panel called the turn-slip indicator. It is a small needle on top of a ball that indicates whether you are in a coordinated turn. It is seldom used, because in a jet most turns are coordinated. When the small needle moves, it does indicate that you are in a turn, but again, you don't know how much of turn you are making.

Working as a team, and with the student as determined as I was to stay in that airplane, we used three secondary instruments in different parts of the cockpit to fly the jet down through the weather. It was difficult and stressful, and a couple of times the jet almost got away from us, but with intense focus, a lot of sweat, and pure determination, we got that jet back to the base.

As the broadcast journalist Paul Harvey used to say on his radio program, "And now—the rest of the story." We later received the Air Training Command Safety Award for the safe recovery of an emergency aircraft.

BUILDING DETERMINATION THROUGH PERSISTENCE

I have illustrated how I was tested and what I had to do to overcome real-life challenges while I was a pilot. You can also develop a mindset of determination to perform to the very best of your ability, even when the situation is tough. The reality is that most people won't live up to their abilities and develop that mindset to nurture and grow determination to achieve excellence in their life. It's sad but true. And what is truly unfortunate is that most people can develop a mentality of determination because it doesn't require any unique talents or skills. It only requires persistence. Just read President Coolidge's quote again.

The good news is that we have already covered some of the essential characteristics of determination earlier in the book.

1. ATTITUDE

A strong positive attitude is essential in building the power of determination, so it's crucially important to avoid self-pity and other negative thinking. Those thoughts will only serve to be a drag on your persistence and can even cause you to give up on your goals. An explicit and confident decision has to be made that you will do what is necessary to weather the storm. You have to be committed to landing at the destination and completing that segment of your achievement journey. You have to make the *conscious decision* that you *will* accomplish your goals. And here is a core fact: Once you have made that uncompromising commitment, the toughest part of the process has been completed. Actually getting there is only a matter of time.

2. STICK WITH THE PLAN

Especially when the weather gets rough. Former heavyweight champ Mike Tyson said, "Everybody has a plan until they get punched in the face." So accept that you are going to get punched in the face. And as I've stressed before, it doesn't matter who you are; that's just a natural part of life. But don't let a temporary course deviation change your route and keep you from flying the intended plan. It's hard to be determined when you don't know where you are going. You can't build the determination to arrive at your destination by flying circles in the sky. This is why in Part III of this book I stressed the importance of constructing a good Flight Plan.

It's likely that times and circumstances may occasionally require a change of direction. But that change should be the result of a deliberative and thoughtful process and not because things have gotten hard and you are giving up or taking the easy way out. If you have built a good plan, clearly understand your reason *why* you are doing what you are doing, and have confidently defined what success means to you, you'll be better fortified to persist when the going gets tough, and you'll have the motivation to keep flying toward achieving your goals.

3. BE SELECTIVE

There are a lot of things that most of us would like to do, but alas, we'll probably never be able to do them all. Limit your choices to just a few important things that really fire up your engines. You want to narrow your focus on those goals that produce the greatest return on your investment of time, effort, and resources. Having just a few major goals at a time will help you stay motivated and help cultivate that determination mindset.

4. BE FLEXIBLE

It is important to have a well-developed Flight Plan and to stick to the plan when times become challenging. In general, organization and consistency are important aspects that help build determination. Yet you don't want to become rigid and uncompromising in your approach to life. You want to embrace spontaneity and flexibility and be open to change. When you are determined to get to your destination, you understand that a different approach may sometimes be required to achieve your results. Thinking in new and different ways may help you come up with new solutions, enabling you to advance in a more favorable direction. Progress and positive momentum increase both your motivation and determination to stay focused on accomplishing that goal.

5. DEAL WITH REJECTION

I spoke at a conference once and shared the green room with a gentleman named Jia Jiang. Jia had spent one hundred days going through what he calls Rejection Therapy, where he would ask people to do or allow him to do some unusual, even crazy things, expecting that he would get rejected. He told me his goal was to desensitize himself from the pain of rejection and to help him overcome his fear. Because of early life experiences, he had gotten into the habit of running away from situations where he feared rejection.

The results of his experiment were phenomenal. Most important, he helped himself immensely in dealing with his fear. But he also began to learn, through trial and error, how to get some people to actually grant his unorthodox requests. The upshot was that he gave a TEDx Talk, which has been viewed over five million times, wrote a book about those one hundred rejection events, and has spoken to audiences all over the world about those experiences, which was why we were in the green room together that day.

Rejection can be disappointing at best and hurtful or even

devastating to some. The first step in using rejection as nourishment for determination is to be honest with yourself and acknowledge that fact.

The next critical step is your reaction to the pain. Building determination requires you using that pain as motivation to take some positive action that makes you stronger. Understand that someone's opinion of you doesn't define who you are. And just because you get a "no" doesn't necessarily mean the game is over. Learn from that rejection, just as Jia did, and use the experiences as the motivation to become even better and stronger as you take on the next challenge.

6. BE PATIENT

Understand the value of patience, because it often takes time to go from point A to point B. In this era of instant gratification, patience is in danger of becoming a lost art. The reality, however, is that most successful people understand the value of delayed gratification because the larger rewards usually take time to achieve.

Being patient enhances your personal willpower and makes self-discipline stronger. It gives you the desire and the power to confront and overcome obstacles and ultimately endure. Having patience reinforces the reality that life is like an airplane; it has its ups and downs. It gives you the understanding that if you keep pursuing the goal over time, it will eventually become your reality. Continuing with some significant presidential quotes, here is one that is right on point from John Quincy Adams, our sixth president:

> Patience and perseverance have a magical effect before which difficulties disappear and obstacles vanish.

7. DEVELOP DISCIPLINE

I said that determination can be developed in most people because the ability is there. The problem is, the discipline is not. Yet research clearly shows that our perceptions about willpower greatly determine the amount of discipline we have.

An article in the *Stanford Report*[17] cited a study by Stanford psychologists showing that people who believed that they had strong willpower performed better in a series of tasks than those who believed their willpower was limited. Additionally, the research showed that the students who believed they had more willpower performed better at sticking to their goals than the group of students who believed that their willpower was limited. The researchers' conclusion was that people have a greater ability to regulate their behaviors than they think.

As is the case with most qualities we would like to possess, the first and most important step is to make a strong commitment to yourself to develop that quality. The choice should be easier when you realize that discipline and self-control are the foundational pillars for the determination mindset.

I'll make a very simple statement that I have both researched and found, through my personal experiences, to be absolutely true: Most of the things that we would like to have in life are available to us. We only need to decide that we want them and to have the determination to see things through.

---

17 Brooke Donald, "Willpower Is in Your Mind, Not in a Sugar Cube, Say Stanford Scholars," *Stanford Report*, August 27, 2013, https://news.stanford.edu/news/2013/august/willpower-study-sugar-082713.html.

DUNKIN' DONUTS

I was on schedule to develop my fast-food network using my SOAR + T goal-setting process. It was time to open another Subway to stay on track with my year-end goals. We had opened several Subways around Boston at strategically located sites, and the airport was my next intended target. It would be the perfect location, and the Delta Air Lines terminal was my calculated objective. As a Delta pilot, I knew firsthand the foot traffic that was generated in the terminal, and I knew it would be a location that I could easily keep my eyes on. I made an appointment with the appropriate Massachusetts Port Authority office to discuss the process of building my next Subway store.

To my surprise and chagrin, the Port Authority didn't directly control the food vendors at Boston's Logan Airport. They had previously negotiated a ten-year deal with Host Marriott to operate all food concessions at the airport. I would have to deal with Host if I wanted to have my Subway at Logan, so I made an appointment with the Host Marriott manager and went over to share my plan.

To say that it was an educational meeting would be quite the understatement. I learned that Host was a franchisee that had national agreements with several major franchisors and had locations in airports all over the country. For example, at Logan, there were Burger Kings, Pizza Huts, Dunkin' Donuts, and Cheers bars, all operated by Host as a franchisee. My pitch to the manager, Bob, was that Subway would be the "healthy alternative" and we should do a deal, with Host subletting some space to me. Bob's response was, "If we want to do a Subway, Host could become a franchisee. We don't need to deal with you." And that was my very first "no" from Bob.

continued

When I got back to my office, I immediately called Subway World Headquarters to see if they had or were negotiating a national agreement with Host Marriott. They did not have an arrangement and had no intention of establishing one. I called Host and made another appointment with Bob.

On my second visit, I made my pitch again, stressing the Subway healthy alternative to all of their current greasy fast-food options. I made the case that we would be increasing market share rather than cannibalizing his. Host could get additional rent and potentially even share profits, which would be a win-win for us both. I also told Bob that Host couldn't do Subway without me, as Subway had no national agreement with Host and was not interested in starting one.

Bob listened respectfully before once again saying no. This time, the reason was that my one-off proposal didn't fit his business model, and it wouldn't be suitable for his Logan operations. I told him I thought he was making a mistake but respected his decision. I also asked if I could keep in touch in case circumstances changed. I think just to get rid of me, he said yes.

From that day on, I made it a point to periodically stop by Bob's office when I was at the airport, usually to pick up mail from my Delta box or to take care of some other company business. I would just pop into the Host Marriott suite, look in his office, and say, "Hey, Bob, are you ready to do that Subway yet?" He'd say no and wave me away. Over time, the nos started piling up and it got to be a joke, and he would laugh as he waved me away.

I arrived back in Boston early from a Delta trip one day, and before going home I decided to stop by Bob's office for what had become our ritual refrain. I stuck my head through his office doorway and said, "Hey, Bob, are you ready to do that Subway yet?" It was the first time he had ever seen me in uniform, as I had, unintentionally, never mentioned that I was a Delta pilot before. He asked, "You are a pilot? I thought you were operating Subways." I told him that I was aggressively growing my Subway operations and running some other businesses as well, but my passion was flying, and I had worked for Delta for a number of years. Bob was intrigued, wanted to know more, and invited me to the Cheers bar upstairs for lunch. That was the beginning of us getting to know each other better and building a more substantive relationship.

A few months later, Bob called and asked me to stop by his office the next time I was at the airport. When I did, he showed me a location where he thought a Subway might work. Another airline was considering renovating its business lounge, and this new space would be created as a result. I told him it would be perfect, and I would have some plans drawn up for the space. He cautioned me not to spend much money, as this was not a done deal, but I told him Subway would draw the plans as a part of my franchisee agreement.

Well, the club renovation fell through and we were both disappointed, but Bob's attitude had now shifted. He said, "It may take a while, but we are going to find some space for the Subway." After almost two years of repeated "no," Bob had now become an advocate.

Then I got the call from Bob that I had been waiting for. Or at least that was what I thought when my assistant told me he was on the phone. But Bob hadn't called to tell me that we had finally gotten space for the Subway. Instead, he said he was being transferred by Host Marriott and, unfortunately, would be leaving soon. He did offer to set up a lunch with the woman who would be replacing him so we could bring her up to speed on what we were trying to do.

continued

I was deeply disappointed. After all the time and effort to build a relationship with Bob and to finally have us working together to get that location, I was crushed to see it all slip away. I appreciated Bob's lunch offer, but given our history and the time it had taken to get to where we were, I wasn't confident that the new manager would easily adopt our agenda.

The three of us eventually had lunch, but the chemistry didn't seem to be there, and the reception to my idea was polite at best. I left the lunch expecting that I would have to build a new relationship all over again, with this time being even tougher than before. I did follow up with a call a couple of months later, but Bob's replacement was still getting a handle on her new position and told me she would reach out if she had anything to share. The situation didn't seem very promising, but after so much time invested, I couldn't just walk away from that airport opportunity. I began to rack my brain on how I could get her to be more amenable to the Subway project.

Surprisingly, two months later, I got her call. She wanted me to attend a meeting with a couple of representatives who were visiting from Host Marriott's headquarters in the D.C. area. I was excited that after almost three years, we were finally going to move on the Subway location at Logan Airport.

At the appointed time, I came prepared with my updated pitch and all of my Subway data. When the meeting began, however, there was no discussion of Subway at all! The HQ guys started talking about Dunkin' Donuts and whether I might be interested in acquiring their locations at the airport.

I was not enthused. I was a Subway guy and focused on growing the number of my units. I didn't want to go to another franchise school and learn a totally different system. Besides, I had done my research before deciding to go with Subway and knew that Dunkin' Donuts was a more complex and expensive operation. My excited high upon coming to the meeting had now dropped to a disillusioned low. I kept a poker face and listened to their pitch without expressing my disappointment. We agreed to have a more in-depth meeting a month later, but I had already decided that this deal was definitely not for me.

At our follow-on meeting, they came with the financial data and the structure of their proposed deal, and I came prepared to respectfully decline their offer. It has been my practice from experience over the years to listen first before I speak. It was a practice that served me well that day.

The HQ guys shared all of the financial data and laid out the structure of the deal. I did some fast mental math and quickly realized that the profit opportunity greatly exceeded what I would expect to make with a Subway location. I was becoming much more interested, as I thought through how I could pull together the required financing to make the buy. And then the universe rewarded my determination. As the icing on the cake with a cherry on top, they offered to finance the acquisition deal over an acceptable period of time. My attitude about becoming a Dunkin' Donuts franchisee changed 180 degrees. I was now all in!

I guess in a technical sense, after a three-year effort, I had failed to accomplish my goal of getting a Subway at the airport. Yet because of not giving up on the struggle, I had been rewarded with an even better opportunity that proved to be much more lucrative and significantly expanded my food service business. My relatively small victory in the grand scheme of life had once again proven the rewards of sticking it out, being resolute, and having a firmness of purpose. In short, of being determined!

History has given us innumerable examples of how people with perseverance and determination have literally changed the world. Consider the journey of Nelson Mandela, who spent twenty-seven years in a South African prison determined to see his homeland a free country. What some may not know is that he had been given the opportunity for freedom on several occasions if he would renounce his views, but because of his principles, he turned the offers down. And the universe ultimately rewarded his determination with freedom on his own terms. South Africa became a free country, with Nelson Mandela becoming its first freely elected president.

Or consider the story of the Wright brothers, two men with a vision that people could fly. Their pursuit of this outrageous idea was considered by many to be pure lunacy. No one believed that controlled, powered flight was possible, so the idea was amusing and whimsical, but nothing to be taken seriously by any sane person. Besides, these brothers were not noted engineers or prominent university professors. They were just two guys who never finished high school and ran a bicycle repair shop.

But following their plan, they built their machine and tried to fly. And they failed. With dogged persistence, they built another machine and tried to fly, and again they failed. In fact, they failed numerous times before finally achieving the miracle of powered flight on December 17, 1903. And though few, if any, realized it at the time, the world had changed and would never be the same again.

UNDERSTAND AND REMEMBER

Look at the legacy the Wrights' determination has rewarded us with today. We have military piloted aircraft that can fly over three times the speed of sound and giant airliners that can carry more than five hundred passengers to locations all around the world. Their persistence at Kitty Hawk ultimately led to the establishment of NASA and space exploration, the Space Shuttle program, and the International Space Station—and because of the determination of Orville and Wilbur Wright, man has walked on the moon. The space program produced consumer products that we could hardly function without today: the personal computer, cell phone cameras, and running shoes, to mention just a few.

The most important thing to understand and remember is that no matter how many times you fall or fail, the only thing that counts is getting up, dusting yourself off, and continuing to move forward. The power of determination has changed, is changing, and will forever change the world.

BELIEVE YOU CAN FLY

"The reason birds can fly and we can't is simply that they have perfect faith, for to have faith is to have wings."

—JAMES M. BARRIE,
Scottish novelist and creator of Peter Pan

RALPH WALDO EMERSON, the great philosopher, essayist, and poet, wrote, "A man is what he thinks about all day long." My CliffsNotes version of his statement would be, "Control your mind, and you control your destiny."

The power of belief has been a fundamental part of our existence from time immemorial. It has been discussed, written about, and experienced for eons. Whether it's belief in a higher religious being and the power of prayer or a belief in the power of positive thinking for self-improvement, belief is a remarkable concept that has affected and guided billions of people at some level through-out the ages. More recently, medical trials have shown measurable benefits in the treatment of Parkinson's, osteoarthritis, and mul-tiple sclerosis, based on patients' beliefs.[18] While the science of belief in the medical or healing context continues to evolve and the causes, including the power of the placebo effect, are just beginning to be understood, the results are undeniable. Belief is a truly powerful force.

WHAT IS BELIEF?

The concept of belief is a state or habit of mind in which we place trust or confidence in someone or something. It essentially encompasses the notion that something can and will happen, even when you don't know how, when, or where it will occur.

Over the years, I have had friends, and even airline passengers, who tie their power of belief with their experience of flying on a plane. Most people don't know how or why an airplane can fly, and in fact, many think it's truly a miracle that the huge mass of metal can even get off the ground. Yet when they get on an airplane, they suspend whatever doubts they may have, and they believe it will take off. And they believe that they can fly thou-sands of miles to their destination without understanding the science and engineering of how it happens. And they arrive, as they believed they would. While their lack of scientific knowledge of the how and why of the flying experience is real, their "belief" is true to them, because belief is the confidence in the truth or the

---

18 Jo Marchant, "Heal Thyself: The Power of Mind over Body," *New Scientist*, August 27, 2011, https://www.newscientist.com/article/mg21128271-600-heal-thyself-the-power-of-mind-over-body.

existence of something not immediately susceptible to rigorous proof (unlike the physics of flying, which, of course, is susceptible to rigorous proof).

WHERE DOES BELIEF COME FROM?

Our belief systems come from a number of different sources, and some are more fixed and impactful than others. No one is born with beliefs, so the environment that we are reared in and the influences of our parents likely form the foundation of many of our initial defining beliefs. According to Wikipedia, over 99 percent of the world's population is affiliated with some religious sect, and I expect that most people in the world hold their religious beliefs as a result of their parental and environmental influences. Around 70 percent of US citizens identify as Christians,[19] and I would guess that most of the people reading this book can complete this sentence: "Now I lay me down to sleep . . ."

Our parents loved us and wanted the best for us as we were growing up, which is why they guided us to accept the belief systems that most likely had been imposed upon them. But, alas, as time passed, we began to develop beliefs of our own. Some of the early beliefs that we were taught just didn't stand the test of time as they related to our individual lives. The Tooth Fairy, the Easter Bunny, and Santa Claus come to mind.

Personal experiences also play a role in our belief mix, including our early school days and childhood friends when we are most susceptible and impressionable. Many of the beliefs we may still

---

19 "Religious Landscape Study," Pew Research Center, https://www.pewforum.org/religious-landscape-study/.

hold dear today were likely adopted at a very young age. I went to Catholic schools from kindergarten through the eighth grade, and at the time, that experience had a major impact on my belief system. Between home, school, team sports, and the Boy Scouts, I had a pretty potent mix of beliefs after my first thirteen years on planet Earth. Belief in the importance of education, physical fitness, and respect for others, especially my elders, came from these different influences. Couple that foundation with a healthy dose of the common social norms, and my belief system was fairly set by the time I entered high school.

WHY BELIEF IS SO CRUCIAL

Our belief system is fundamental to how we approach life, the expectations we develop, and the potential for the success we will achieve. A close friend, Charles Siplin, who became a key mentor in my midtwenties, gave me a book early in our relationship titled *As a Man Thinketh*. This now classic, best-selling self-help book, written by British philosopher James Allen and published in 1903, was inspired by chapter 23, verse 7 from the Bible's Book of Proverbs: "As a man thinketh in his heart, so is he." The book served to reinforce a belief system that I had already embraced from my parents' exhortations that I could be anything I set my mind to.

Allen described his book as "dealing with the power of thought, and particularly with the use and application of thought to happy and beautiful issues. . . . It shows how, in his own thought-world, each man holds the key to every condition, good or bad, that enters into his life, and that, by working patiently and intelligently upon his thoughts, he may remake his life, and transform his circumstances."

The book begins with the following statement:

> Mind is the Master power that moulds and makes,
> And Man is Mind, and evermore he takes
> The tool of Thought, and, shaping what he wills,
> Brings forth a thousand joys, a thousand ills: —
> He thinks in secret, and it comes to pass:
> Environment is but his looking-glass.

Allen's message is simple: We are what we think and believe we are. He believed that powerful thoughts, pointed in the right direction, are the foundation and base on which all happiness and success are built.

While Allen approached the importance of thought and belief in attaining great success from a philosophical viewpoint, a commonsense perspective takes us to the very same destination. Most of the actions we take and the things we do, or choose not to do, are preceded by our thoughts about them. It naturally follows, then, that every great action, accomplishment, and achievement in history was preceded by inner thoughts that led to those results.

I shared in Chapter 5 that one of my all-time favorite books is *Think and Grow Rich* by Napoleon Hill, which I have read at least fifteen times over the years. I have found valuable nuggets and great insights in that classic that I have successfully applied to my own endeavors. Hill's quote, "What the mind of man can conceive and believe, the mind of man can achieve," is particularly powerful and has been used as the key to success by some of the wealthiest titans of industry in American history.

In essence, the more you think about and believe a certain thing, the more you will focus and concentrate on it. The more you are focused on it, the more it becomes a part of your actuality and the greater your chances of achieving it. What you truly believe is then possible for you and ultimately becomes your reality in life. And if you are focusing on the belief that you can achieve a specific goal, you are engaging in one of the fundamental keys to actually achieving that success.

We are going to be at our very best when we have a strong fundamental belief in what we are doing. Some of the greatest athletes of all time have stressed the importance of believing in their abilities to accomplish the extraordinary feats achieved during their professional careers. While they in no way minimize the importance of dedication, discipline, and hard work, they have emphasized the importance of the unshakable belief in their talents as a critical factor in their phenomenal success.

Michael Jordan is recognized by many as the greatest basketball player to ever play the game. When the game was in the final seconds and his team was a basket behind, he believed that he would make the game's winning shot, and he did it more than twenty-five times in his career. "I've always believed that if you put in the work, the results will come," Jordan is known to have said. Jerry Rice, the greatest wide receiver in NFL history, believed that when he ran his pass route down the field, he would catch a touchdown pass, and he did it more than anyone else to play the game—197 times.[20] Tiger Woods is the most dominant golfer to ever hit the links. He has made some of the most spectacular shots in golf history and holds numerous PGA records. Belief in himself and the ability to make that shot has been the key. "There's no

---

20 "Players: Jerry Rice: Career Stats," NFL.com, http://www.nfl.com/player/jerryrice/2502642/careerstats.

sense in going to a tournament if you don't believe that you can win it," Woods says. "And that is the belief I have always had, and that is not going to change."

"You are what you believe yourself to be."

People act in a manner consistent with how they see themselves. In effect, you are what you believe yourself to be. If you have self-limiting beliefs, you will be limited. If you have high expectations and expect to succeed, most often you will. People who strive for excellence have a high degree of self-confidence and great personal belief. That's what keeps them going. Even when the *how* is not clear, their *will* to succeed is 100 percent. You have got to believe in order to succeed, and the more you achieve, the greater your belief that you will continue to succeed. Success actually feeds on itself, and the rewards that come are more than tangible ones. The end result is increased self-confidence and feeling better about yourself.

HOW TO BUILD BELIEF IN YOURSELF

One of the keys to a strong sense of belief is high self-esteem. People with high self-esteem like and respect themselves. They appreciate their own value and worth. People with low self-esteem have no direction, lack purpose, and have a fear of failure in achieving goals. If you want to achieve at a high level, a good starting point is to increase your self-esteem, which is the catalyst for changing an undesirable belief system about yourself, and the key to breaking the psychological bonds that may be holding you back.

FOUR STEPS TO POWER UP YOUR SELF-ESTEEM

1. Take a candid personal inventory.

Think about and define your strengths and list the things that you are particularly good at. At the same time, be candid about your flaws or weaknesses. You'll want to maximize the opportunities to showcase your strengths, as these will rapidly propel you ahead and increase your confidence. If possible, minimize or avoid situations that may emphasize your weaknesses. While we may understandably want to improve on our faults, time and effort are usually better spent going from good to excellent rather than from poor to mediocre.

2. If you have it, get rid of the victim syndrome.

It may seem easy to transfer blame for your shortcomings to someone or something else. I expect we all have heard a litany of excuses at one time or another—and used a few ourselves: "I'm not getting ahead because . . . I'm black . . . I don't have enough money . . . I didn't go to the right schools . . . I never have enough time." To be clear, I'm not suggesting that we don't have legitimate challenges that we all have to deal with. As you increase your personal belief in yourself, you won't need excuses and you'll be able to face your challenges directly.

3. Step up and take responsibility.

Why are you *really* where you are in life? The answer to that question is actually very simple: Because of you. You are responsible for what you have done in the past, where you are now, and where you will eventually be. Once you accept this fact and take responsibility for your destiny, you instantly empower yourself to take control of it. Like the often spoken quote says, "If it is to be, it's up to me."

4. Be judicious in listening to others.

Everybody has an opinion. But not all opinions are valuable or even appropriate for you. You'll have to consider the source, the person's expertise, and their motivation for offering their opinion about you or what you should do. You'll want fact-based, objective advice. Evaluate the advice and weigh any information that is directed toward you. You are the captain of your flight, and you alone have to be comfortable with the decisions you make and, ultimately, who you are.

GETTING OUT OF YOUR COMFORT ZONE

Thinking big and pushing yourself to get out of your comfort zone are bona fide ways to build a strong sense of belief in yourself. Have you ever wondered why all companies, organizations, and people don't perform at high levels of excellence? Because most don't truly *believe* they can. I'm sometimes asked what it was like to go to a service academy. My answer is immediate and always the same. The Air Force Academy experience taught me that I could do much more than I ever *believed* I could. We were *forced* to do more, like the time spent in a simulated POW camp, and quite honestly, if I had been left to my own devices, I may have failed the task. But failure wasn't an option at the Academy, so surviving those experiences built a tremendous amount of self-confidence. You leave the Academy believing that there isn't much in life that you can't accomplish if you just decide that you want to. But you don't have to go to a service academy to build a strong sense of belief.

I was with a dear friend some years ago as she was reviewing her small business's year-end results and setting her revenue goals for the next year. For the closing year, she had averaged over $5,000 a week and was setting a goal for the coming year of $7,000 a week, about a 40 percent increase, which, granted, was an aggressive goal. I asked, "Why not set a goal of $10,000 a week?"

> *"Change your beliefs, and you*
> *can change your life."*

Her immediate response was, "I could never do $10,000 a week. That would be double what I am doing now." I told her I believed she could, and more important, if she believed she could, it would happen. We went through several scenarios of what it would take to double her revenue. She could add a higher-revenue service to her current offerings, and with increased marketing she could pick up an additional one or two customers a day. This could result in 260 to 520 new customers in the next year. After our discussion, she began to think about the possibilities in a different way. By the end of that next year, a $12,000 week was a slow week for her business. She had literally changed her thinking and produced wealth beyond her initial beliefs. It's no cliché to say, "Change your beliefs, and you can change your life."

DEVELOP A GROWTH MINDSET

Another way to build belief in ourselves is to develop a growth mindset. Dr. Carol Dweck of Stanford University has been studying human motivation and achievement for more than thirty years. Her work focuses on why some people succeed and others don't. Her concept of the growth mindset verses the fixed mindset shows how our belief system determines what is within our control when we want to nurture success.

Dweck's book *Mindset: The New Psychology of Success*, originally published in 2006, shows how our thoughts and beliefs "affect what we want and whether we succeed in getting it." As she lays out a compelling case for how our most basic beliefs determine our ability to achieve and grow, she delves into the neuroplasticity quality of our brain, which is the ability of our brain to change and grow. People with the two different mindsets achieve dramatically differing results. Those with a fixed mindset believe that the skills we have are what we were born with and that we have all the talents we are ever going to have. Because we were born with a level of intelligence or certain defined skills, we cannot change them. The ability to change, learn, and grow is limited, if we can even do so at all. A person who says, "I'm not good at math," or "I'm not a good dancer because I wasn't born with rhythm," indicates someone with a fixed mindset.

People with a growth mindset, however, believe that we are the captains of our own jet and we can fly it wherever we choose to go. We can choose the skills that we want to master, and our hard work and effort determine how and to what degree they can be developed and improved. Those with a growth mindset have a strong belief that they have the capacity to learn, cultivate, and grow the skills that they choose to pursue.

FIVE STEPS THAT WILL HELP YOU ACHIEVE A GROWTH MINDSET

1. Replicate your past.

You've got this because you have done it before. I've already used the example of how you learned to walk as a baby, but there are many more examples you can choose from. Did you learn to ride a bike or roller-skate as a kid? Then you have already shown the potential for a growth mindset. You developed and improved on new skills that you chose to learn. Realize that you can do it again.

2. Continue education.

Education is the foundation for both personal and professional growth. Read books, play the piano, learn a new language, or go to your local college and take a course. The deeper our knowledge base, the more value we bring to the world around us, which in turn increases our opportunity for greater all-around success.

3. Accept challenges.

News flash! Life can be tough at times. We have either just solved a problem, are dealing with a problem, or getting ready for a new problem. When I was dealing with a challenge early in my life, my dad would say, "It builds character." He was right: It actually did. Dealing with problems develops grit, and overcoming challenges instills a sense of pride and confidence, which are fundamental traits for long-term success.

4. Be open to feedback.

No one is perfect, and we all make mistakes. Even when we are doing things right, most of us can improve on our performance. Understanding what we did wrong or how we can do better and accepting that feedback in a positive rather than a defensive way is the foundation for personal growth.

5. Work your brain.

Dr. Michael Merzenich is considered to be the father of neuroplasticity, which is the ability of the brain to change itself. In his 2013 best-selling book, *Soft-Wired*, he explains that the brain contains a series of circuits and pathways and that the neurons in our brain create new pathways when we do novel and different things. The more we repeat a new activity, the more the neurons fire and the activity begins to become "soft-wired" in our brain. The often quoted phrase coined by neuropsychologist Donald Hebb says, "Neurons that fire together wire together." Dr. Merzenich tells us, "You are designed to be continuously improvable . . . at virtually everything you do." And the most amazing thing is that the more you improve yourself by acquiring new skills, the more you simultaneously improve your brain's wiring mechanisms or its ability to get better, at anything and at any age. Neuroplasticity of our brain is truly a fascinating and wonderful quality and enhances the growth mindset.

POSITIVE AFFIRMATION: TELL YOURSELF YOU'RE GOOD

Muhammad Ali once said, "I figured that if I said it enough, I would convince the world that I really was the greatest."

Positive affirmations like "I believe in my skills and abilities" have an important role to play in building the belief in ourselves. They have been shown to help us believe in our potential to accomplish a feat that we desire to achieve. And there is both scientific research and psychological theory behind the benefit of positive affirmations.[21] Just like doing new things, affirmations have been shown to increase the neuron wiring in our brains by the release of dopamine. MRI data has revealed increased activity in the prefrontal cortex of the brain as a result.

Telling yourself that you will achieve what you desire has the effect of convincing your conscious and subconscious mind that it can actually happen. If you say it enough, you will begin to believe it. Besides, a positive affirmation costs you absolutely nothing, and if others have been shown to benefit, why can't you?

YOU CAN DO IT

The benefits of having a strong belief in yourself are completely real. The self-esteem, confidence, and conviction you build are key components to achieving high levels of sustainable success in life. When you believe in yourself, you'll make the effort and put in the work to do the things necessary to accomplish your goals.

---

21 C. N. Cascio, M. B. O'Donnell, F. J. Tinney, M. D. Lieberman, S. E. Taylor, V. J. Strecher, and E. B. Falk (2015), "Self-Affirmation Activates Brain Systems Associated with Self-Related Processing and Reward and Is Reinforced by Future Orientation," *Social Cognitive and Affective Neuroscience* 11(4), 621–629.

Even more important is the determination that flows from a strong belief in yourself. When faced with difficulty and seemingly insurmountable challenges, this belief gives you the willpower to continue to forge ahead. When you experience the inevitable setbacks and you get knocked down, belief in yourself gives you the drive to get back up and continue the journey—because you are determined to arrive.

During Air Force pilot training, a part of our syllabus required me to fly my jet solo to a remote base, do three touch-and-go landings, and then return to my home base. I had flown to Spence Airport several times before but always with my instructor pilot and usually in the mornings when the visibility was clear. This would be the first time I had flown there by myself. I took off and headed west, with the summer sun in my face. The South Georgia haze made it almost impossible to see my reference points on the ground, and I couldn't locate the checkpoint where I needed to make the turn to get to Spence. When I realized I was lost, a mild panic began to set in.

I knew that I could use my instruments to return to the home base, but if I didn't complete the Spence Airport mission, it would be a major failure that would put my training status in grave jeopardy. Becoming a jet pilot was my dream, and I had already put too much time and effort into the program to see it all go away. So, I began to talk to myself, out loud and with conviction: "You can do this, 'T.' You can do this! You've done this flight several times before. Pull it together and find that damn point! You can do this!"

Knowing I had gone well beyond where I was supposed to make the turn, I started to turn the jet around to backtrack the route I had taken. As I rolled out in the opposite direction, it was like a curtain had been lifted! With the sun now at my back, the points on the ground were crystal clear. I was able to find the turn point, get to Spence Airport, and complete my landings. Believing in myself had given me the motivation to put the panic aside and keep flying that mission. Belief had kept me from giving up and returning to the home field and putting my dream of becoming an Air Force pilot at risk.

An excellent way to hone your command of belief is to use the power of visualization to see yourself doing what you believe you will do. This is not voodoo science, and it is a concept that works. Air Force and other professional pilots use it to "chair fly" their missions before they ever get in the plane. Top athletes use it to see themselves achieving at higher levels and even breaking world records before they have even begun to perform. Jack Nicklaus, one of the greatest golfers to have ever played the game, has been using visualization for decades. Nicklaus has said, "I never hit a shot, not even in practice, without having a very sharp in-focus picture of it in my head."

CREATE YOUR FUTURE

It has been said that the best way to determine your future is to create it, and the power of your belief is what is required to make that happen. If you don't believe in yourself, how can you expect someone else to believe in you? You have to believe that you are more than you ever imagined and better than you now think you are. Believe that you can do more, have more, and be more, before you will ever get what life has out there waiting for you.

This is a subject I am passionate about because I know it to be true. You can achieve excellence in your life by believing in yourself, developing a growth mindset, and setting big goals. How do I know? Because I have flown that route myself. Look at my early resume: A black kid from a small southern town with the deck stacked against him. I wasn't born with any special gifts or talents, and though I worked hard, I was never number one in my class or the best athlete on the field. But I had the gift of parents who instilled in me a belief that I could do whatever I wanted to and be whatever I wanted to be. I believed, I decided, I took action, and I became a pilot, a lawyer, a businessman, and a leader.

Though I'm not very religious these days, I do believe that the biblical verse Mark 9:23 from the Sermon on the Mount is universally applicable: "If you can believe, all things are possible to one who believes."

CLEARED TO LAND

> *"If you can walk away from a landing, it's*
> *a good landing. If you use the airplane the*
> *next day, it's an outstanding landing."*
>
> —CHUCK YEAGER,
> first man to fly faster than the speed of sound

WRITING THIS BOOK has been a remarkable journey for me. I hope reading it has been an enlightening one for you. My journey had its roots in two sources and some personal observations. First, I've often been asked how I have been able to do the diversity of things I've done professionally—being an airline captain for a major carrier and a lawyer/businessman at the same time. Second, after telling some of the stories that have been included in this book to family and friends in casual conversation, the reaction was everything from "Wow, I had no idea" to "You've got to write a book and share some of those things." I'd laugh off those suggestions and quip something like, "Yeah, I'll get around to it one day."

Well, the time finally arrived. As I pondered an answer to how I had been able to be a success as a pilot and lawyer/businessman, I realized that I had used the same process, time and time again, to accomplish every personal and professional goal I had set for myself. Initially, my approach had been unwitting, but over time it had developed into a consistent and repeatable process. I hope that by sharing my approach, I might be able to help others move to higher levels of accomplishment in their lives.

THE P4 SYSTEM

I named my approach the P4 System because each of the salient points begin with the letter P. It was not a complicated process that I sat down and developed after a rigorous academic effort. It was a result of reflecting on what I had consistently done, over time, to get the things done that I wanted to accomplish. I've also been able to help others by sharing my approach in the past, and this book gives me the opportunity to connect with a larger audience. Let's review the components of the P4 System.

PRINCIPLES

First and foremost, as a result of the influences of my parents, Catholic schools, great coaches in team sports, and becoming an Eagle Scout, I developed a strong sense of right and wrong. And even though I haven't always agreed with my parents, and I don't subscribe to some fundamental aspects of Catholic doctrine, and scouting has changed dramatically over the years, collectively, those influences shaped a simple philosophy that I strive to live by: Do the right thing, for the right reason, and in the right way.

This philosophy is also the first and most important tool in my leadership toolbox. It was my mantra in my entrepreneurial ventures, boards that I've chaired, and in leading the Association of Graduates (AOG) at the Air Force Academy. It goes without saying that things happen that are often unanticipated and over which you have no control. And we all make mistakes. But I've always told the people I've led, "If you are doing the right thing, for the right reason, and in the right way, I've got your back 100 percent, even when things go sideways." And that is why Priniples became the first P in the P4 system.

PEOPLE

I've been blessed with two great parents, and when I say blessed, I really mean that. I have close friends who didn't have great relationships with their parents or didn't have both parents for very long. I was lucky—and also smart enough to listen to what they had to say (at least most of the time). I took my mother's words to heart when she cautioned me about who my friends should be, especially when I saw some of them get into pretty serious trouble.

My years at Orangeburg High also gave me a keen insight into people's character. There were very few white students who stood up to the tremendous peer pressure existing in that racially charged setting to be polite to me and to treat me as a fellow human being. I developed a deep respect for the few who did, mostly some of my fellow football teammates.

My Air Force years, particularly my time at the Academy,

cemented for me the importance of having topflight people in my life. My Academy class, lightheartedly known as the "Illustrious Class of '73," was a tight-knit group and has been one of the most successful classes to come through the Academy. The class produced more three- and four-star generals combined than any other class to date, a NASA astronaut, one of the wealthiest businessmen in the Academy's history, and a president of the AOG. The quality of the friendships I established and the talent and character of the people who are my friends have been second to none. This is why People is the second P in the P4 System.

FLIGHT PLAN

I learned the value of having a plan in high school when I was forced to navigate the racial challenges and circumstances of those days. That plan allowed me to survive and then thrive in that environment. A plan was also critical when I worked to become an Eagle Scout and when my dad and I discussed my college options. The plan brought home the fact that I'd have some serious work to do if I wanted my ambitions to extend beyond the local black college. I've used the same process in every major endeavor I've undertaken, and it has consistently worked to produce the desired results. This is how Plan became the third P in the P4 System.

PERFORMANCE

Performance is often the simplest part of the P4 System. Performance basically means just this: You have to do the work to get it done. Note: I didn't say it's the easiest part. But it's the simplest. Let me use a short analogy to illustrate this point. If your car breaks down on an eight-lane highway at rush hour and causes a major traffic jam, the solution to get traffic moving again is simple—move your car off to the side of the road. If you do not have a tow truck or someone to stop traffic and help you push the car off to the side, that simple solution won't be accomplished very easily.

The truth is that most of what you'll need to reach a goal is not intellectually challenging. In most cases, it just takes the discipline to go out and complete the job, and the discipline comes from making the goal your priority. Law school was not intellectually difficult, but the number of legal cases and other material that had to be read was voluminous. It took giving up going to the clubs, and the parties, and skiing or the wine country on the weekends to get the work done. Running fast-food franchises was not intellectually difficult. You went to the company schools to learn the systems, and then it took the discipline to run them like you were supposed to. In effect, doing the work means doing the right thing—which brings us full circle back to Principles. And that is why Performance is the final P in the P4 System.

STORIES AND OBSERVATIONS

I debated whether I should use my personal stories or other examples to illustrate some of the points that would validate the efficacy of using the P4 System. I didn't want the book to be an autobiography or to come across as one. But I didn't want the examples to come across as information I had just studied or read. I felt that sharing real-life examples of things that I had actually experienced would ultimately be of greater benefit to you.

My observations have taught me the following:

1. *Most of what we need to deal with in life is not complicated.*

I've said this before, but repetition is the mother of excellence, so it bears repeating. Most of the effort to achieve those things in life that are important to us and that we set as goals do not require being a genius or having other unique gifts. Persistence is the key. Recall the quote that was attributed to President Calvin Coolidge about persistence, which resonates so strongly with me:

> Nothing in this world can take the place of persistence.
>
> Talent will not: nothing is more common than unsuccessful men with talent.
>
> Genius will not: unrewarded genius is almost a proverb.
>
> Education will not: the world is full of educated derelicts.
>
> Persistence and determination alone are omnipotent.

I have experienced this personally in so many different aspects of my life and have found it to be consistently true. Showing up and hanging in there are more than 80 percent of the game. It is not that complicated. It is just as simple as that.

2. *It is the little things we can do that make a huge difference.*

And it really is the little things in life that make a tremendous difference! We were taught to say "please" and "thank you" and to try to keep a smile on our faces. It is truly amazing how those little things can advance your position in life. We were taught to keep our rooms clean and to make our beds, and something as simple as that has literally been the foundation for changing the world. I would highly recommend googling Admiral William McRaven's speech, "If you want to change the world, make your bed."[22] Admiral McRaven led the US Special Operations Command when the United States captured Saddam Hussein and killed Osama bin Laden, two world-changing events. Admiral McRaven gives a wonderful short synopsis on why doing the little things are so important in life.

The overwhelming majority of people don't understand #1 and #2 above, but these are simple and fundamental facts. That is why excellence is so elusive and mediocrity prevails.

Most of us want to look and feel good, live a long life, and have money in the bank. Eating less and better, taking a daily walk, and saving and investing only 10 percent of your income each month would, over time, go a long way toward achieving all those goals. I'm reminded of the story of Anne Scheiber, a little old lady who worked for the IRS. She lived in a one-room apartment in New York City and never made more than $3,150 a year. She lived to be 101 and died with a portfolio worth over $22 million. If she could do that, why can't you? It's not that complicated, and the little things do make a difference.[23]

3. *Excellence and being the exception.*

The Dictionary.com definition of *excel* is generally something like "surpass others or be superior in some respect or area; to outdo; do extremely well."

---

22 "Adm. McRaven Urges Graduates to Find Courage to Change the World," *UT News*, May 16, 2014, https://news.utexas.edu/2014/05/16/ mcraven-urges-graduates-to-find-courage-to-change-the-world.

23 James K. Glassman, "An Old Lady's Lesson: Patience Usually Pays," *Washington Post*, December 17, 1995, https://www.washingtonpost.com/archive/business/1995/12/17/ an-old-ladys-lesson-patience-usually-pays/ec000053-d7bf-4014-b841-546bd5847a80.

My personal definition, adopted from my dad, rest his soul, is to do your best, each and every time. He used to say, "Son, success in life is seldom the result of your aptitude or your talent." He was a schoolteacher during the early part of his career and earned two master's degrees. Notwithstanding his educational achievements, he would say, "Success is not even about educational level or more than average intelligence. What it is about is a commitment to excellence." He would tell me, "William, if you do your best, you'll do better than most, because most people aren't going to give you their best. Most people aren't committed to excellence." And if you meet my dad's definition of excellence, you will surpass the dictionary's definition by easily outdoing others and doing extremely well.

You can be the exception to the mediocrity that most people settle for by consistently doing your best. We can all do that. Strive for excellence and you can earn that promotion, get that new job, or start your own business. You can accomplish more in life than you ever thought, believed, or realized you could.

I know this because I have done it myself. I have applied the P4 System to achieve some amazing things: flying faster than the speed of sound, flying in the cockpit of a jumbo jet, becoming a lawyer and one of the few attorneys who can argue before the Supreme Court of the United States. I've built a multimillion-dollar business and turned around a major association while taking it to new heights. I also raised two wonderful daughters, have been actively involved in my community, and have answered the call to serve in government for four governors, two each on both sides of the aisle.

The most important point to reemphasize is that I have achieved these results without having been born with a silver spoon in my mouth and without being blessed with any unique gifts or talents. I have achieved my success by following the principles presented in this book, and you can do it too! The power of choice lies solely with you.

I wish you all the best on your Flight to Excellence, as you soar to new heights in business and life!

ABOUT THE AUTHOR

WILLIAM "T" THOMPSON is a former international airline captain, lawyer, award-winning businessman, and professional speaker. A former association president and CEO representing 50,000 colleagues, "T" has also worked for four governors on both sides of the aisle, overseeing state aviation agencies. He has been featured in *The Wall Street Journal*, *Black Enterprise* magazine, *The Boston Globe*, and the *Atlanta Business Journal* and has appeared on NBC, CBS, and PBS, among many other media outlets. "T" lives in the Atlanta area, and his proudest accomplishment is raising two wonderful daughters who are focused on living lives of excellence.